D0772309

Reschooling the Thoroughbred

Peggy Jett Pittenger

With Foreword by

Hugh Wiley

The Russell Meerdink Company Ltd.
Menasha, Wi 54952

Library of Congress Cataloging-in-Publication Data

Pittenger, Peggy.
    Reschooling the thoroughbred / Peggy Jett Pittenger
    Includes bibliographical references and index
    ISBN 0-929346-09-2: $23.95

    1. Thoroughbred horse--Training. I. Title

SF293.T5P5 1990
636.1'32--dc20   90-9142
                                              CIP

Published by The Russell Meerdink Company LTD.
P.O. Box 485
Menasha, WI 54952 USA
(800) 635-6499 In the USA & Canada
(414) 725-0955 Worldwide
(414) 739-4322 (FAX)

Printed in the United States of America

For Jean, again

Acknowledgements

I am grateful to the following people for assistance in preparation of this book:

Mark Foley, D.V.M. of Keswick Equine Clinic, Gordonsville, Virginia, for reviewing the material on unsoundness.

John Strassburger, Editor, *The Chronicle of the Horse,* for lending file photos.

Rhonda Williams, Editorial Department, *The Blood-Horse*, for locating esoterica.

Hugh Wiley, Oak Hill Farm, for reading the text of this book in manuscript.

And all the generous people who allowed us to use their treasured photographs in this book.

Table of Contents

Olympian Hugh Wiley Aboard Master William

Hugh Wiley was a member of the distinguished United States Equestrian Team of 1956 and 1960. The medal winning team dominated international show jumping of the era. The team won the prestigious Prince of Wales Cup at the London International Horse Show an unprecedented three years running.

In 1958, Wiley won the King George V Cup on the gray Thoroughbred, Master William. He won the King George V cup a second time the following year on Nautical, in addition to the Horse and Hound Cup and the Daily Mail Championship, all at White City with Nautical.

The Triumphs of Hugh Wiley and Nautical were celebrated in the Walt Disney film, "The Horse with the Flying Tail.."

Also a successful breeder of Thoroughbreds at his farm in Maryland, Wiley bred the outstanding puissance star Thoroughbred, Ksar d'Esprit, ridden by Bill Steinkraus. (Photo courtesy of Hugh Wiley)

Forward

Many enthusiastic riders have a limited background with horses. Unless you were raised on the farm with our four legged friends, you have a long row to hoe. Basic horse sense can be developed over the years with experience and hard knocks, but most of us, unfortunately, want to just climb aboard and take off. This taking off can be a frightening episode so I suggest strongly that you read a great deal and proceed cautiously.

Peggy Pittenger's "Reschooling the Thoroughbred" is a book that will be a helpful learning experience and a future guide to all its readers. For me, this delightful book brought back memories of learning the hard way. Peggy's no nonsense and easy to understand approach to horse sense will save you valuable time in finding and bringing your new horse up to snuff. I only wish that I had had such a book as this when I started my equestrian career. Why go through the struggles to rediscover the do's and don't's of bringing your horse along. Reschooling the Thoroughbred brings out the subtleties of good training coupled with the patience that will give your horse the chance to understand and develop to his fullest.

Most buyers are hoping to find that special horse. Whatever your experience, I would be willing to bet that there is a suitable horse for you somewhere out there. They come in all shapes, sizes and colors so be prepared to take the time to search out and find the animal that is just right for you. I prefer the Thoroughbred with a good mind. They are very sensitive, respond to pressures and will accept training. The dictionary says that a THOROUGHBRED is bred from the purest and best blood; high spirited, mettlesome, elegant, graceful and thoroughly trained. The latter is up to you. Good luck and I hope this book will be your guide.

Hugh Wiley

Oak Hill
June 29, 1990

Introduction to the Updated 1991 Edition

In 1966, the original edition of *Reschooling the Thoroughbred* was written as a guide to the selection and retraining of the ex-racehorse for pleasure riding and for the show ring. The Thoroughbred is bred for athletic ability and is a talented, versatile horse that can master any discipline. The fact that there were many sound, willing retired racehorses available for new careers prompted the writing of that book. The 1966 edition of *Reschooling the Thoroughbred* has been out of print for many years. Today there are more retired racehorses than ever looking for new careers and riders looking for the horse of their dreams. This new edition of *Reschooling the Thoroughbred* will guide a new generation of riders in the selection and training of their Thoroughbreds.

There have been many changes in the horse world during the twenty-five years since facts and figures for the original edition of *Reschooling the Thoroughbred* were collected. Generally, the quality and sophistication of riding in the United States has vastly improved and has been widely disseminated. Much credit for improved riding and management skills is attributable to the growth of the United States Pony Clubs, which are modeled after the Pony Clubs in Great Britain, an offshoot of the British Horse Society. Opportunity to participate in horse shows, both at the recognized and schooling levels has expanded so that there is scarcely a weekend of the year when it is not possible to participate. Trail riding, polo and combined training are also expanding their scope.

Meanwhile, the number of Thoroughbred foals registered annually has more than tripled, in response to increasing racing days, expanded purses and a runaway market; there was an exhilarating escalation of Thoroughbred prices, for both bloodstock and racing prospects in the early 1980's followed by an equally precipitous decline in prices in the mid-to-late '80's. Encouraged by a market in which it seemed to be virtually impossible to lose money, foal production was amplified in unrealistic anticipation of continued soaring prices; animals, which in a saner time would never have made it to the breeding shed, glutted the sales with their mediocre progeny as people with no background in nor love of horses were helping themselves with both hands in the expectation of making a killing in the wild and unrealistic market. The relationship between price and projected earnings at the track widened and stretched to the breaking point. The market went into a sharp decline. Nowhere was the shake out felt more keenly than at the bottom. Well bred horses of good conformation were still bringing good prices, although nothing to match the glory days, while the middle and lower portions of the spectrum were hit very hard. This situation, overproduction of Thoroughbred stock coupled with the vagaries of the market, has held the cost of a suitable Thoroughbred prospect for reschooling to very much the same level as it was in 1965, with little or no allowance for the general inflation in prices and wages in the intervening years. It is still very much a buyer's market.

In recent years European Warmblood horses have become a major factor on the American scene. As the term implies, these horses have been bred in Europe strictly as sport horses for dressage, show jumping, eventing and hunting. The type has been developed by selective breeding from Thoroughbred and draft horse crosses. Horses must meet certain demanding criteria to earn inclusion in their respective stud books. Warmbloods are called by many names: Selle Francais, Oldenburg, Trakehner, Wurtenburg, Hanoverian, Rhinelander, Holsteiner, Dutch Warmblood and Swedish Warmblood. Generally speaking, these horses are large, kind, calm, athletic and phlegmatic, well suited to the tasks for which they have been bred. They are also exorbitantly expensive.

Thoroughbred racing is filled with many terms and customs which may baffle those who are unfamiliar with them. Some of those terms and customs appear in this book and to make the going easier, a few explanations are in order.

First, an asterisk (*) always precedes the name of a horse which was imported into the United States. For example, the outstanding broodmare sire *Princequillo is designated as an import by the asterisk.

Second, it is customary to note the sire, dam and dam's sire whenever mentioning the name of a Thoroughbred. For instance, a mention of Secretariat (Bold Ruler-Somethingroyal by *Princequillo) looks like this. Bold Ruler was the sire and Somethingroyal the dam of Secretariat. *Princequillo (an import) was the sire of Somethingroyal.

Finally, the term "start" means that a horse actually ran in a race. If a horse had 10 "starts", he participated in 10 races. A horse is said to have "finished in the money" if he finished first, second or third in the race. Finishing in second place is known as a "place"; finishing in third place is known as a "show".

Disclaimer

The purpose of this book is to acquaint the reader with the opportunities which exist in purchasing and reschooling Thoroughbred racehorses. The information is drawn from the author's extensive experience working with Thoroughbreds and should be advancing the knowledge of the amateur horseman.

However, it is not all-inclusive and is not intended to cover every situation which may arise. Each horse is an individual with its particular characteristics and traits, therefore the reader should use caution and discretion in following the methods discussed in this book. The author stresses safety in working around horses. However, accidents can happen even to the experienced horseman. Therefore, to reduce the chance of injury to either the horse or handler, proper equipment in good repair must be used at all times. Under no circumstances should any horse be ridden unless the rider is wearing a securely fastened, approved safety helmet.

The experience, temperament and attention of the handler, as well as the temperament of the horse, are the determining factors in the element of risk of injury. Therefore, neither the author nor the publisher make any representations or warranties, either express or implied, that injury will not occur when following material in this book, and assume no liability therefore.

Chapter 1

The Secret of Finding Bargain Thoroughbreds

Suppose you were made the following offer: The owner of a racehorse asks if you will buy his perfectly sound, beautiful, 4 year-old Thoroughbred for only $500, or about 50¢ a pound. Three years ago, he bought the horse as a yearling for $75,000. Since then, he has spent another $ 48,000 on training. When you tell him you don't have $500, he offers to give you the horse free in exchange for your promise to give it a good home.

Does this sound too good to be true? If you are like most other horsemen, you'll believe that there has to be a catch somewhere. Nobody in their right mind would make this kind of offer. But the fact is that these types of offers *are* made almost every day at every Thoroughbred racetrack in the world. The supply of ex-racehorses looking for good homes greatly exceeds the number of knowledgeable horsemen willing to take them.

Many are called but few are chosen. Approximately half of all Thoroughbreds fail to make a single start, probably because their training moves have not indicated that they are fast enough to win. Of the horses who do race, only half ever win a race of any kind. Among those who race and win, the majority do not earn back their training expenses. Therefore, the horse who "pays his way" must be considered to be a superior performer. With average annual earnings per starter of only $8,500 and average training expenses of $16,000 per year, one hopes to make up the deficit by the earnings of a stakes winner, but less than 3% of all runners attain stakes-winning status. In recent years, foal production has outstripped the number of racing days, making the chances of breaking even more remote than it was in the past. The harsh financial reality of the racetrack makes thousands of young Thoroughbred horses available at ridiculously low prices. If a racehorse has not attained success by the end of its third or fourth year, its value as a racehorse plummets to almost nothing.

You must understand that the difference between a fast racehorse and a slow one is miniscule. A Thoroughbred which can run a mile or more at a rate of 12 seconds a furlong (a furlong is 1/8th of a mile) is worth hundreds of thousands of dollars. Secretariat is the only horse that has ever run the Kentucky Derby at a rate of less than 12 seconds a furlong. A horse which runs at 13 seconds a furlong, a mere 8% slower, is virtually useless as a racehorse. It is unlikely that you have ever traveled at the rate of 13 seconds a furlong on the back of a horse even on those terrifying occasions when your mount was running away with you. What is "slow" on the racetrack is mighty "fast" around most stables.

Although these racehorses are sold simply because they are too slow, there is a great deal of prejudice among many pleasure horses people against off-the-track horses. Ex-racehorses are believed to be too "hot" for other purposes. They are all mistakenly thought to be suffering from one unsoundness or another. The rigors and regime of the track are said to make them unsuitable for reschooling. This is not the case.

Such prejudice serves as a great injustice to thousands of beautiful, well-mannered and sound Thoroughbreds which are unable to make a living on the track. The very things which make a Thoroughbred unsuitable for racing may make him a perfect horse for your purposes. A horse which lacks the aggressiveness to race may make a perfect trail horse. A horse which doesn't like the bumping and shoving of the racetrack may make a careful jumper. The stride which makes him slow may be just the stride needed to compete successfully in dressage.

Not only are ex-racehorses suitable for reschooling, they are actually preferred by many knowledgeable riders. Olympic champion three-day-event rider Bruce Davidson has won many medals on the backs of former racehorses. According to Canadian Jim Day, Olympic Gold Medalist and Sovereign Award winning trainer, "If a horse's legs have stood the pounding and the grind of racing without any major flaws or injuries, and his brain stayed intact, the chances are that he could be a very solid, very useful horse for show purposes . . . Over the years he ought to wear better and have a more durable set of legs just from the conditioning he has received as a racehorse in training early in life."[1]

Arthur Hawkins of Bedford, New York, a leading judge, trainer and seller of top quality show hunters and jumpers prefers to buy horses from the racetrack. He says, "They are better looking, better balanced, and better in their movement than the half or three-quarter Thoroughbred hunter of the old days (warmbloods). They are naturally more athletic with long, flat strides with no waste of motion. The half-bred just doesn't move with as long a stride over a hunter course . . . he'll be somewhat plainer in the head and thicker in the neck, or have some other portion of his body that is not as elegant as the Thoroughbred's."[2]

If you are seeking to "move up" to a Thoroughbred you should begin by exploring the opportunities and bargains that await you at your nearest racetrack. It is at the racetrack that you will find a horse that can be reschooled for any purpose and which can be purchased at a price to fit almost any budget.

---

[1] Jim Day quoted by Rita M. Jefferies, "*Easing the Transition from Racetrack to Show or Pleasure Barn,*"(Canadian Thoroughbred Horse Society, Rexdale, Ontario, 1990), p.12
[2] Arthur Hawkins quoted by Harlan Abbey, "Substitute Careers", *The Thoroughbred Record,* Lexington, Kentucky, Sept. 6, 1969.

Joe Fargis and Ex-Racehorse Touch of Class

The obscurely bred Stillaspill (Yankee Lad-Kluwall by Cornwall) foaled in 1973 raced to expectations, finishing unplaced in 6 starts at 2 and 3. She passed through a series of sales barns in Pennsylvania, before being found by Joe Fargis who recognized her extraordinary jumping ability. That jumping ability was fine tuned to perfection under patient handling. "Patience is the big word," in reschooling former racehorses, says Joe Fargis[3] who finds no problem in converting former platers to world class performers. Renamed Touch of Class, the brilliant mare under Joe's skillful ride became only the second USET performer to win an individual Olympic gold medal.[4] The mare is still a good one, winning Grand Prix classes in her late teens.

[3] Joe Fargis, Southampton, New York, telephone conversation, June 1990.

[4] John Strassburger, "Great Jumpers of the Past," *The Chronicle of the Horse,* Middleburg, Virginia, March 2, 1990, p. 12.

Chapter 2

What Becomes of Slow Racehorses

In 1989, the average price for a Thoroughbred yearling sold for racing purposes at public auction was $32,905. The majority of these horses will never attain success at the racetrack. Within a few years, thousands of these high-priced yearlings will be sold for a few hundred dollars or, in some cases, be given away to good homes.

The number of Thoroughbred foal registrations has increased astronomically in recent years because of the growing popularity of racing (see chart on following page). Since the 1940's, more and more states have legalized pari-mutuel wagering. In states where racing had already been established, the racing season has been lengthened. In the past twenty-five years, the number of horses actually running in races (as opposed to merely training in preparation to race) has nearly tripled. The turnover is tremendous. As runners fall by the wayside due to injury or demonstrated unsuitability to racing, new hopefuls move in to take their places.

What becomes of the horses whose racing days are over?

Outstanding entire (ungelded) horses - the cream of the crop such as Alydar or Secretariat - are retired to stud where they live lives of more than oriental splendor. They are pampered and pleased, groomed to a shine, stabled in elegance, overfed, admired by all and paid court by visiting dignitaries and the general public. Each year, 40 or more of the choicest and most impeccably bred mares will visit the breeding sheds of these

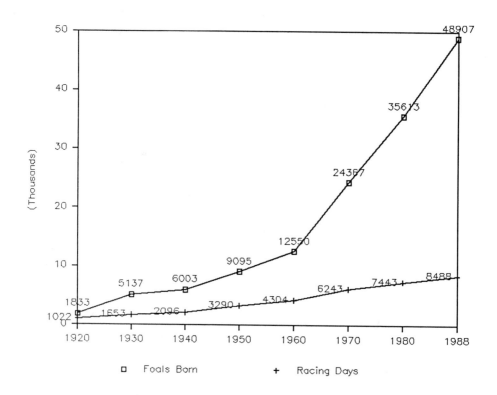

| | Foals Born | | + | Racing Days | |

Increase In Thoroughbred Foal Registrations

Between 1920 and 1960, Thoroughbred foal registrations increased at a rate paralleling the increase in racing days. During this time, approximately three foals were registered for each day of racing offered in the United States. A steep climb in the number of foal registrations began in 1960. By 1988, almost six foals were registered for every day of racing offered. This increase in foals has resulted in a surplus of Thoroughbreds which cannot make a living at the track. This surplus presents an opportunity for anyone to acquire a reschooling prospect at a bargain price. (Data for graph courtesy of the Daily Racing Form).

chosen stallions.

Upon the death of popular stallions, tears and bourbon flow freely as the racetrack stars of the past are buried beneath the greensward, the spot often marked by a larger than life-size bronze statue. The Man O'War funerary statue has been moved from the original burial site to the Kentucky Horse Park in Lexington. The Bull Lea statue still dominates the horse cemetery at Calumet Farm.

Less distinguished colts that are well bred or the near relatives of first class performers, may also be given a trial at stud. Even a few unraced or non-winning colts are given a chance to prove themselves as stallions if they have shown promise while in training, have illustrious ancestors not too remote on both sides of their pedigree, are of unusually imposing conformation or if they are blessed with sentimental and optimistic owners.

The optimism was certainly justified in the case of movie-mogul Louis B. Mayer's *Alibhai (Hyperion-Teresina by Tracery) who proved to be that rarity: an unraced leading sire, his progeny earned three and a half times the national expectancy. Bred by the Aga Khan, *Alibhai was purchased at a yearling sale in England. The colt was taken to California where he displayed great brilliance but broke down, bowing a tendon in training at two, before he had ever started. The brilliance he had shown in his works as well as his distinguished lineage, justified trying him at stud.

At Mayer's farm in Riverside County, California, there was assembled "as fine a band of mares as any to be found at any US Thoroughbred nursery".[1] No doubt, the opportunity afforded *Alibhai of being bred to such a distinguished band of matrons, did much to enhance his success at stud. At the dispersal of the Mayer Thoroughbred holdings, *Alibhai was sold to a syndicate headed by Leslie Combs II of Spendthrift Farm near Lexington for $500,000, a record at that time.[2] In his lifetime at stud, *Alibhai sired an impressive 57 stakes winners.

---

[1] Neville Dunn, "Mayer Dispersal," *The Thoroughbred Record,* Lexington, Kentucky, Feb.1, 1947.
[2] William H. Robertson, *The History of Thoroughbred Racing In America,* (Englewood Cliffs, New Jersey: Prentice-Hall, Inc., 1964), p. 406

Mundane winners are not likely to lead the glamorous life. They will have neither a numerous nor a select harem. In fact, they will probably spend more time siring hunter prospects and keeping the local 4-H mare and foal projects in production than in siring potential racing stock.

Successful race mares also are assured of green pastures and superb care for as long as they continue to produce high quality offspring, often well into their twenties. Today, when offered at auction, champion mares bring prices in the millions. Lady's Secret, racing's all-time leading female earner sold in 1989 for $3.8 million. Her stablemate, 1988 Kentucky Derby winner Winning Colors, sold in the same sale for $4.1 million. Even unraced and unplaced fillies are in demand if they are by fashionable sires or are from solid, producing families.

A few conscientious and affluent owners pension off their former runners. Calumet Farm kept champion Bewitch as a pensioner until she was twenty, even though the only foal she ever produced did not live. She is buried alongside her distinguished relatives near the statue of her sire, Bull Lea. But for the most part, racehorses must sing for their supper, or earn their keep doing something else for a living. Geldings, undistinguished colts and non-producing mares, however, have no guarantee of leading a life of privileged ease after retirement from the track. Most racehorse owners have neither the money nor the desire to support a non-productive horse.

Although rarely discussed in print, the fate of horses whose racing days are over is an embarrassment to the Thoroughbred industry which likes to present itself to the media in the most upbeat manner possible. Disposing of the former racehorse is not a subject of discussion in Thoroughbred publications. Their disposal is the dark side of the moon, the other side of the coin, of an industry which wants only its shining, glamorous face presented to the public. What a shame that horses who have given the full measure of their strength, youth and courage should be consigned to the scrap heap as another replaceable item in our disposable economy. The situation is a disgrace to the sport of racing, and further, it is a pity that the powers that be have failed to address the situation and have done little to rectify this waste.

Due to the hazards of racing of young horses, the occurrence of unsoundness in some is inevitable. In certain cases, humane destruction is the only feasible course to follow. A severely crippled animal is no pleasure to himself or to anyone. Some horses are temperamentally unsuited to a life other than racing. It is better that they be put down rather than risk injury to other horses and riders. But the sad truth is that thousands of young, healthy, intelligent, serviceably sound horses go directly from the racetrack to the slaughter house. They are the "meat and meat by- products" in the pet food you feed to your cat and dog. What a waste of talent!

I have heard it said that the cruelest thing one can do with a used-up racehorse is to give him away to "a good home." The rational of the above statement is that the "good home" may not turn out to be so good. Picture the horse who received the finest care when he was a potential money earner, now kept in a muddy barbed-wire enclosure, underfed and neglected, except when some kid takes him out and runs his legs off. This situation is changing. The educational programs conducted by both the U.S. Pony Clubs and the 4-H, whose horse projects often outnumber all other animal projects combined, have helped to reduce poor horse management at the backyard level.

The State of New York, at its Walkill Correctional Facility, a minimum security prison, has a program where retired racehorses are used in prisoner rehabilitation. The inmates learn riding and stable skills to enable them to find employment in the Thoroughbred industry upon their release from custody. The Thoroughbred Retirement Foundation, a non-profit organization, operates the farm where the horses are kept and instruction is given.

In 1963, we bought the 3 year-old Thoroughbred filly Mi-Gal-Sue (Hearts Away-Miss Gallo by *Bernborough) for $35. She was on her way to be fed to the lions and tigers at the Pittsburgh Zoo. She was reschooled and ridden for pleasure by our 15 year-old daughter Nancy. The pair served as models for many of the photographs in the original edition of *Reschooling the Thoroughbred*. Although the filly had ringbone and osselets, she

21

never had a lame day with us. She produced 11 handsome foals, show and race winners, failing only once to conceive during her productive years. She lived to be 25. Among her produce: Chief Counsel, stakes placed winner of 12 of 140 starts; and National Hunt Race Association Timber Horse-of-the Year, Champerty, winner of 14 races in 48 starts on the flat, and 32 of 37 starts over timber, setting two course records.

A growing number of retired racehorses are finding second careers after learning new skills. Quite a few stay on at the racetrack as stable ponies where their speed and "can do" attitude make them very useful. At the racetrack, the term, "pony," is used to designate a calm, dependable horse, usually a gelding, who goes out on the track as a companion to a racehorse. The rider of the pony leads the racehorse with the chain of the shank passed over the runner's nose, or through his mouth, if he is particularly rank. A horse is "ponied" when the trainer wants the horse to exercise without the weight of a rider on his back, or he may be trying to get the horse fit himself without the added expense of a rider, an exercise in futility since the horse's back muscles must be conditioned to carry a rider in a race. Rather than leading the racehorse, the pony may just be ridden beside him to inspire confidence and good behavior. If the race horse is going to breeze or work, the pony boy or girl will use a leather strap looped through the bit, rather than a shank, galloping along until the furlong marker where the work is to begin. Then the strap will be slipped from the runner's bit so he is free to break off at that point. Then the pony picks his horse up again at the end of the work, jogging back to the gap, the wrong way of the track, on the outside rail.

Many horses are taken to the saddling paddock before a race and from the paddock to the starting gate by the faithful stable pony. Going to the post with a pony saves the jockey's strength for the actual race, rather than having him expending his energy trying to control a head-strong horse who might try to run off in the post parade. Any horse which can master theses skills will certainly make a good pleasure mount.

Other retired runners spend their lives as equitation instructors at camps and riding schools and at public livery stables where the capability of going the extra mile endears them to their owners. Many find their way to the hunt field, polo grounds, Pony Club, show jumping ring, dressage arena, three-day eventing, or serve as all purpose trail and pleasure mounts. Some go on to become international champions in such things as jumping, three-day eventing and dressage.

Although one does not customarily think of Thoroughbreds as harness horses, this is another area in which the breed excells.

In the days before the Civil War, Porter Rockwell of Salt Lake City, had a contract to provide coach horses for the Butterfields Stage Lines which passed through Utah; his stock was selected for their superior speed, strength, endurance and durability. The horses which Mr. Rockwell provided were all bred by him from a herd of Thoroughbreds he had brought to the West from Kentucky.[3]

Fully 90% of the horses used by the United States Park Service Mounted Police are Thoroughbreds, former racehorses, donated to the Park Service. Although geldings are used most frequently, there are four entire horses serving in the unit stabled near Washington, D.C.

Amateur riders are beginning to learn what champion equestrians have known about ex-racehorses for many years. Olympic rider, Bruce Davidson, says "I prefer a former racehorse to a youngster that has been left to grow too fat and soft . . . if they hold up to the rigors of racing chances are they will hold up for whatever I want them to do."

"A perfect example," continues Davidson, "is Might Tango (by Mighty Mine out of Bettango). He was raced as a two/three year-old and then we . . . started his training as a four-turning-five-year- old and in two years he won the Individual World Championship at Lexington in the Three Day Event. He was very successful at the Advance level for quite a few years. Most of our youngsters race first and hunt, show or event later in life. Getting a young horse fit (hard fit) is to me much better for

---

[3] Bill Taylor, "Those Versatile Thoroughbreds, Then and Now," *The Oregon Horseman*, Eugene, Oregon, August, 1984.

them in the long run."[4]

In discussing Might Tango's racetrack background, Bruce Davidson says, "I think a competitive background tells you much about the horse in the long run...if a horse is properly fit early in life, it will carry him on. If he has raced and is still sound, I think that's the most wonderful vetting you could ask for. It's more than we are going to do for the rest of his life.[5]

According to show jumping star Dennis Murphy, "I favor two things about the Thoroughbred. First, I believe they are faster in a jump off and secondly, I honestly think a Thoroughbred is more durable...Look at the records of such horses as Jet Run, Idle Dice, and Southside (American Thoroughbred show jumping stars)...those horses jumped big jumps for years and years. I think a Thoroughbred horse is bred to be more of an athlete at this level of show jumping." He states that the qualities people boast about in their expensive European bred sport horses "are Thoroughbred features."[6]

After being tried and found wanting at the racetrack, there are thousands of young Thoroughbreds available annually at a price to fit any budget. These are quality animals whose ancestry in every line can be documented for over 200 years. Who of the human race can claim the same distinction?

In becoming the owner of a Thoroughbred, you become part of the colorful panoply of kings, queens, oriental potentates, merchant princes, riverboat gamblers, lords and ladies, knights of the realm, sheiks of Araby and Dubai and other highflyers, all the way back to the Bedouin chieftains who have held the breed of running horse in high esteem. You will be buying a horse with magical qualities. His perfection at the gallop is the product of rigorously selective breeding. He has telepathic sensitivity to his rider's wishes, so that the horse and rider seem as one. Sitting upon a Thoroughbred striding smoothly without apparent effort, you seem to glide over the land, controlling the power beneath you by the merest tightening of a finger or the slightest shifting of weight in the saddle. A Thoroughbred is an

---

[4] Bruce O. Davidson, Chesterland, Unionville, Pa., letter May 14, 1990.

[5] Nancy Jaffer, "Second Chance," *Spur*, Middleburg, Virginia, July/August 1990, p.112

[6] Cooky McCung, "Dennis Murphy Finds a Special Reason to Return," *The Chronicle of the Horse*, Middleburg, Virginia, March 2, 1990.

incomparable delight and the reason why many of the world's great riders are not satisfied with anything less.

Bruce Davidson & Might Tango Ride To Victory
Bruce Davidson, the first in history to win consecutive World Three-Day individual titles, brushes through the towering "Bullfinch" on Might Tango in the steeplechase phase of the competition. Might Tango received 61.4 in dressage, 12.0 time penalty points in cross-country and had two rails down in stadium for a total of 93.4 penalty points to prevail over Cambridge Blue (Ireland-120.6), Ladaloo (Germany-122.8) and Sergeant Gilbert (USA-123.4). (Thomas photo courtesy of the Chronicle of the Horse.)

Alf Landon Won Big on the Track and in the Show Ring

Alf Landon (Times Roman-Galanya by Galoot) a 1967 bay gelding standing 16:2 enjoyed a successful race career for owner/breeder Landon Knight of Bath, Ohio, winning 19 races, placing second 19 times and third twelve times for earnings of $65,630 in 95 starts. At five, he won the Youngstown Handicap. He was given away at the end of his racing days. In his first retirement home, he was neglected until Sandy Coddington saw him and bought him for $300. Under his talented amateur owner/rider Alf began his winning ways again. In the show ring he won many large classes and several year-end championships including 1984 Central Ohio Hunter Jumper Association Horse of the Year; 1985 COHJA Horse of the Year; 1986 COHJA Horse of the Year; and in 1987 Central Ohio Show Association Open Hunter Pleasure Champion; COHJA Reserve Amateur Rider; COHJA Reserve Horse of the Year. At twenty-one Alf started being shown by 90 pound junior rider Missy Fossesca who has been winning many large equitation classes with him.[7] At last report, at twenty-three, Alf still looks like a four year-old.[8] (Photo courtesy Dianne Mosbacher).

---

[7] John Englehart, "Alf, the Horse With a Heart as Big as his Girth," *Ohio Thoroughbred*, Cincinnati, Ohio, Sept./Oct., 1988, p. 30.
[8] Landon Knight, Bath, Ohio, Telephone Communication, May 1990

Chapter 3

How to Find
Reschooling Prospects

The best place to start looking for your reschooling prospect is at the racetrack nearest to your home. A list of all Thoroughbred racetracks in North America is included in Appendix II to aid in your search.

In states where Thoroughbreds are raised and raced there are local breeders associations, groups of horsemen who usually publish a magazine of local news and/or conduct sales of yearlings and breeding stock. They also promote local farms and horses, support legislation favorable to racing and breeding interests and pass out year-end awards at their annual meeting. A letter or phone call to the breeders association nearest you (See Appendix I) might point you in the right direction to find a prospect for reschooling.

At most racetracks, racing is seasonal. A race meet will be held lasting several months. Then the track will be "dark" until it opens again for another meet. Sometimes horses stable and train at the track during the off-season. Optimism runs high at the beginning of a race meeting. Owners and trainers are reluctant to give up on a horse which still has a chance of earning back some of what has been invested in him. But when a stable is preparing to ship out to a new track, the hope is to get rid of the dead wood, to sell or give away the runners not earning their keep. Rather than continue the large expenses which go with keeping a racehorse, most owners prefer to cut their losses and sell the non-winner at a nominal price, usually at a large loss.

Your first step may be to post a notice listing your requirements on the bulletin board in the racing secretary's office at the track. This will yield the names of numerous people who, indeed, have a horse for sale. The racing secretary's office is visited frequently by all trainers and other racetrack employees. It is usually located somewhere in the grandstand area of the track. It is easily accessible without making any special arrangements. When listing your requirements, don't be overly specific as to your wants. Terms like "good dressage movement" and "hunter prospect" mean little to most racehorse people. "WANTED: big, sound, young mare or gelding" will get results. And, while you are visiting racing secretary's office, plan to stay to watch the races to get a feel for the pageantry and tradition of the sport.

Your next step is to visit the stable area of the track to seek out horses that are for sale. Don't be reluctant to do so because of stories you may have heard about racing. The racetrack has been erroneously painted as a den of thieves and degenerates making emotional and physical cripples out of unfortunate equines in the name of greed. The truth is that the majority of racetrackers are clean living, hard working, family people with the same middle class virtues and values you would hope to find in your next door neighbor. The brutal hours preclude anything else. Racing success depends upon a healthy, physically fit runner with a good mental outlook. The racetrack is a friendly place. It is easy to become acquainted. Conversation is easy with the other "rail birds" who have gathered to watch the horses at their early morning works and gallops. The horse fraternity is a gregarious one. Busy as racetrackers are during the training hours, they always have a few minutes to "talk horse."

The track's stable area is called the backstretch. It gets this name since at most tracks the barns are located along the far side of the track opposite the grandstand, where the home stretch is located. A visit to the backstretch will be productive in finding reschooling prospects. Before visiting the

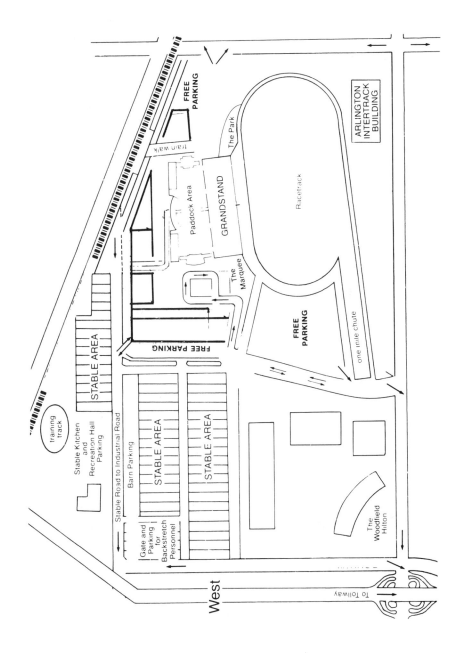

A Typical Racetrack Layout

(Courtesy Arlington International Racecourse, Ltd.)

backstretch, it is helpful to ask a friend who has a horse racing or training there to allow you to visit the barn where his horse is stabled and to meet his trainer. If you do not know a racing owner, try phoning the business office of the track. State your interest in seeing the morning exercise and in looking at horses you might be interested in buying. Ask what procedure you should follow.

Security measures vary greatly from track to track, from lax to stringent. (At Keeneland, you can walk right in. At Belmont, it's easier to get into Fort Knox.) Everyone who works at the racetrack or who has access to the track must be licensed by the state. This includes everyone from the trainers right on down to the parking lot attendants. Every licensee is fingerprinted; anyone with a criminal conviction must state the particulars of his arrest and conviction on his license application. Failure to do so, and the records are checked by the F.B.I., will result in the revocation of the license. No sport is more thoroughly policed than Thoroughbred racing in order to maintain the integrity of the sport and to protect the bettor's confidence in the honesty of the game, which, like Caesar's wife must be above suspicion.

Because of these security measures, it is usually necessary to get a visitor's pass from the security guard at the entrance to the stable area before you will be allowed to enter the area. At only a few tracks, is it possible to come and go without being challenged. Check into the procedures for gaining admission to the backstretch area before you leave for the track.

When you make your trip to the track, plan to get up very early. In most instances, the track will be open for training only from first light until 10 or 10:30 AM. It then closes so that the maintenance crew can drag and harrow the racing surface in preparation for the afternoon's races.

Understanding how the racetrack works will help you make conversation with the people you will meet and make the job of finding your reschooling prospect easier.

Arriving at the backstretch area, you will see ranks of shed row type barns with box stalls back to back. The low pitched roof is extended to make a walking path, or shed row, around the entire barn where horses are cooled out after their exercise, or where a young horse will walk under tack when he first comes to the racetrack. When you stand in the shed row, stand on the side next to the stalls. To stand on the outer edge is to invite a reprimand, since you are likely to be kicked by a fractious or playful horse. A horse is walked around the shed row in a counter clockwise direction and is led from his left side, therefore, he is better able to kick out to his right, or to the outside of the shedrow than to his left, should he feel rambunctious.

The trainer supervises his little kingdom and is responsible to his owners for the success or failure of their horses. The trainer's chores are endless. He must please his owners who are his source of income. The owner of a racehorse pays his trainer a "day rate" plus a percentage of the horse's winnings. Many owners are unreasonable in their demands. Others are ignorant about horses. It is the trainer's job to educate them. He must schedule appointments with the farrier and veterinarian; he must supervise and instruct his assistants; deal with exercise riders and jockey agents; purchase feed and supplies and enter his horses in races for which they are both fit and eligible. He must supervise the gallops, breezes and works of his horses and interpret the often cryptic remarks of the rider. Someone must stay until the last horse from the last race is cooled out and bedded down. If a horse colics, someone must stay with it. The horses in his care must be watered off at night. If there is no night man to give the four A.M. feed, the trainer, or another of his day staff must perform that chore as well.

Racetrackers put in a long day by anyone's standard. They must be up before dawn to lightly groom and tack up the horses in their charge as well as to inspect them carefully for any heat or swellings, lumps, bumps and runny noses. Rectal temperatures are taken daily by many conscientious trainers because a slight elevation in temperature from the daily norm may be the first and only sign that all is not well. The hay net, feed tub and water bucket are also checked since the horse that does not "clean up" may have a problem developing.

The usual morning program of training involves daily slow

gallops of 1-1/2 to 2 miles. Breezes at speeds less than all out are held once or twice a week. Gradually, as the horse acclimates to training, he is asked to go further and faster, but not both in the same work. He is asked for more effort in very small increments. After coming off the track, he is hosed or sponged off, with special attention given to joints and tendons. He is gone over with a sweat scraper and then dried with a towel or linen rubber. He is walked, either in hand or on a mechanical walker, wearing either a wool cooler or a scrim fly sheet depending upon the season. During the walking period, he is allowed only small sips of water. After 45 minutes or an hour, when he is thoroughly cooled out and watered off, he is returned to his stall which has been cleaned and freshly bedded with straw. His water bucket will have been scrubbed and refilled with fresh water and his hay net will have been filled with the best available hay. His legs will be wrapped in standing bandages. Doing up (wrapping), prevents his legs from filling after exercising. He will walk under the shed row, most likely for a day or two after a race or a hard work, rather than going to the track. On days that he does not race, he may be taken out of his stall again in the afternoon and walked around and perhaps allowed to graze if there is grass nearby.

The spectrum of races has been compared to a pyramid with the great majority of races at the base of the purse structure, being claiming races. Most horses run in claiming races. A claiming race is restricted to horses which may be claimed (purchased) at a stated sum, a practice which insures a competitive field of horses of similar ability running against each other. Any bona fide owner who has run a horse at that particular race meeting is eligible to claim another owner's horse for the declared price or to have it claimed for his account. Claiming prices run the gamut from $1,200 at minor tracks to $90,000 or more at "the races" as the more prestigious tracks are called. Claiming races may be further restricted as to age, sex, number of wins, or wins since a certain date.

A higher calibre horse runs in allowance races. Horses in allowance races are not eligible to be claimed. The greater the weight of the jockey, the slower a horse is likely to run. In allowance races, different weights are assigned to various horses in the race in an effort to give horses of differing abilities an equal chance of winning. Weight allowances are based on number of wins or amount of money earned or date since the horse's last win. The conditions may state, "Non winners of a race other than maiden or claiming", or "Non winners of one such race allowed three pounds." Fillies and mares are allowed 5 pounds when racing against colts and geldings.

There are also starter allowance races which are restricted to horses which have started for a stated price or less. There are optional claiming races where horses can be entered to be claimed or not, with the horses not to be claimed carrying a higher weight than those entered to be claimed.

In handicap races, the weight to be carried is assigned by the racing secretary.

There is no entry fee to run in claiming or overnight (non-stakes) handicap races or allowance races.

Stakes races, in which the owner puts up nominating, entry and starting fees which are added to the purse offered by the racetrack, are the highest class of races and the most difficult to win. Only 3% of all Thoroughbreds ever win a stakes race of any sort.

Purses increase with the improved class of the race. At the very tip of the pyramid are the Graded (called Pattern or Group races in Europe) stakes races which are the most prestigious races in the world. They are ranked Grade-1 (the highest class), Grade-2 and Grade-3. Stakes races are run under handicap, allowance or scale weight conditions. As we have seen, allowances are weights assigned based on the horse's past performance with penalties (added weight) for winning and allowances (weight off) for failure to win. The great three-year-old classics, the Kentucky Derby, Preakness, Belmont and Travers Stakes are run at scale weights: 126 pounds for colts and geldings, 121 pounds for fillies.

In scale weights for mixed ages, horses four and up carry more weight than three-year-olds. Two-year-olds race only against their own age group. In races run under handicap conditions, the racing secretary assigns a weight to each horse nominated to the race, a figure based on his assessment of the horse's ability based upon its past performance, in comparison with that of the other horses nominated. The owner/trainer has a right to accept or decline the weight assigned. The idea of a handicap is to put on the track a competitive field of runners by using weight to bring the better horses back to the lesser lights. Handicap stars such as Kelso and Citation met all challenges conceding twenty-to-twenty-five pounds to their less talented rivals.

At the racetrack, almost all horses are for sale at one price or another. Walking up and down the shed rows, you will get a good idea of the type of horse that appeals to you. Look at as many horses as you can; talk to their handlers. Trainers, grooms, exercise riders, hot walkers, and veterinarians can all mention to you a "nice, kind horse with a bad case of the slows" that someone in the very next barn is "just about to give up on" or would "sell right to a good home." Van drivers who haul horses from track to track usually know where there are several prospects available; often they deal in horses themselves.

While you are visiting, be sure to visit the track kitchen. It is located in the backstretch area, often near one of the gaps where horses enter and leave the race or training track. Everyone passes through the kitchen at least once or twice a day to pick up coffee, a sandwich, or a *Daily Racing Form.* Many a horse is trained or handicapped over a cup of coffee in the kitchen. A note posted near the cash register should put you in touch with the owner/trainer of that big, sound, slow horse.

Finding your way around the backstretch and making contact with the people who work there is the easy and fun part about finding a reschooling prospect. The hard part - evaluating the dozens of horses that are for sale - is still ahead.

Cunningham Creek

Allowance winner, Cunningham Creek (Tom Tulle-Algebar by High Drag) a bay gelding foaled in 1983, started 32 times, winning 7, placing second four times and third on 5 occasions for earnings of $51,349. After a life threatening injury, he was purchased by his devoted racetrack groom, Linda Pozo. Dr. Ron Genovese of Randall Veterinary Hospital, advised having him destroyed due to the seriousness of his injury, but Linda's tears persuaded him to attempt surgical repair of the gelding's shattered right knee. After three hours of surgery, the knee was screwed and wired back together and the long recuperative period began: first, four months of stall rest and then more than a year's turn-out. At the end of the rest period, Linda first led Creeker around her yard for a few days and then rode him in the yard for ten minutes or so at a time until they both felt confident and then started out riding the trails. Linda describes him as "a friend and a trail buddy. A big hearted horse who gave me a lot".[1] (Photo courtesy of Rick Pozo).

[1] Linda Pozo, Russell, Ohio, Letter, May 1990

35

Ex-Racehorse Thrives on 100 Mile Rides

Daggit, renamed Dogget, (Son Excellence-Cozy Gal by Crozier) chestnut gelding, 1976, was unplaced in 11 starts. He was bought in 1986, as a ten-year-old, by Rebecca Spicer of Woodsboro, Maryland, after a series of intermediate owners. At sometime previous he had broken his right hind fetlock; although the joint is still enlarged, with care and attention, he remains sound, as evidenced by his activities. He and his owner participate both in dressage shows and in competitive trail riding, including 100 Miles in Three Day Rides in Virginia, New York, Vermont and North Carolina, in addition to numerous other 15 to 50 mile competitions. Additionally, they hunt and whip with the Carrolton Hounds. His owner describes him as "fine and gentle", although rather on the muscle when hard and fit as he must be for endurance riding. (Photo courtesy of Bucky Spicer).

Chapter 4

What to Look For In
A Reschooling Prospect

In looking at a reschooling prospect, you should remember that the same standards of good conformation apply to the Thoroughbred as to any other breed. In checking a Thoroughbred's appearance, it is important not to confuse condition with conformation. A horse in active race training will be lean and hard, all muscle, bone and sinew, without an ounce of excess fat. In sharp racing trim, he will have a tucked-up look and may appear to be ewe necked, especially if he is very young. He will have a general overall air of immaturity, which is not surprising, since a horse is not fully mature until he is five and a half or six years old. The designations of immaturity - "colt" and "filly" - used until the age of five instead of "mare" or "horse" attest to this fact. Geldings are so-called regardless of their age. People who criticize the Thoroughbred for being weedy usually have seen only immature individuals in racing condition; they would scarcely recognize the same horse matured and filled out. Some horses in training weigh as little as 750 pounds while at maturity they may weigh up to 1,400 pounds.

In looking the horse over, first get a general impression of him. Does he please you? If not, better to move on to another. In evaluating conformation, it is easy to lose sight of the forest for the trees. In fact the horse may be forgiven a few minor faults if he hangs together well and is in harmonious balance and proportion. All of his parts should look like they come from the same set, not as if the horse were assembled from an odd lot of spare parts. For instance, the beauty of a good head is nullified if it is poorly set on a coarse neck. A full bodied horse supported by spindly legs is neither pleasing to the eye nor engineered for soundness.

After getting an impression of the horse as a whole, his gesture and expression, it is a good idea to start at the bottom and work up. As the old saying goes, "No foot, no horse." If his underpinnings do not pass inspection it does not matter how classy the rest of him is unless you're looking for a lawn ornament instead of a good ride.

So, begin at the feet. Is the hoof wall dished? This condition is a sign of past or present problems. Are the horse's feet the same size? A smaller hoof indicates a compromised blood supply. Does he wear a bar shoe? A bar shoe is usally applied while a crack in the hoof wall heals. Be alert for thickened pasterns and fetlocks, mushy tendons and round, rather than flat, knees. The various problems to which a racehorse is subject are discussed more fully in later chapters.

Because of the ivory-like density of Thoroughbred bone, a trait inherited from his desert ancestors, he will have a lesser dimension as measured around the fore cannon than a cold blood without being considered to be deficient in that regard. Strength of bone is determined by its density, not its diameter.

Two features which bear no compromise are the shoulder and the hindquarters. A long, sloping, shoulder means a long, smooth ground covering stride, while an upright shoulder produces a short, stilted, jolting gait. The hindquarters furnish the horse's source of impulsion, propelling him forward. Any shortness from the point of the hip to the point of the buttocks should be severely discriminated against because such deficiency will limit his athletic ability. The Thoroughbred appears, at first glance, to be long bodied. Actually, he has a short body due to his having one or two fewer lumbar vertebrae than the common horse, a trait he inherited from his Arabian ancestors. The appearance of length is due to the Thoroughbred's extreme length from point of the hip to point of the buttocks and to the oblique angulation of the shoulder (characteristics due to selective breeding for racing efficiency) so that the Thoroughbred, rather than being long bodied, in fact "stands over a lot of ground."

The Thoroughbred will show greater refinement than other breeds - greater muscle definition, cleaner throat latch, more sharply chiseled facial features, a more prominent withers and a finer, silkier coat than the ordinary horse. He also appears more alert. Many Thoroughbreds have very high withers. In certain individuals there will be a dip where the neck joins the shoulder which no amount of nuchal fat can ever completely conceal. Such a withers furnishes a long attachment for the shoulder muscles and a resulting long stride; the only drawback is that an improperly fitted saddle rubbing on the thinly covered spinous processes can cause a gall at the point of contact. A saddle with a high gullet used with a thick pad will protect the high withered horse from injury.

Over the years the average size of the Thoroughbred has increased from 13:3 hands in the 1700's to almost 16 hands at the present time, yet good ones still come in all sizes. Saucebox, winner of the St. Leger in 1855, was only 14:2, while the only horse to ever seriously challenge the undefeated Ormonde in the 1880's was The Bard who stood a mere 14:3. The filly Good Thing, technically a pony as she stood only 14:1-1/2, was a consistent winner, carrying as much as 121 pounds to victory. Major U. S. winner Dark Mirage (*Persian Road II-Home by Dark by Hill Prince) 1956, at 14:3 and 750 pounds won twelve races, including the Filly Triple Crown and $362,788. One of the most important "good little ones" was Northern Dancer (Nearctic-Natalma by Native Dancer) 1961, winner of the Kentucky Derby in record time in 1964. A compact power house of a racing machine, he stood 15:1-1/4. At stud he is a legend, stamping his progeny with his own prowess and short stature.

At the other end of the scale is the aptly named Whopper (*Pharamond II-Romance by Luke McLuke) 1932, who at that time was probably the largest horse seen in major stakes competitions in the United States. He was not only tall (17:2) [1] but stout, weighing 1,300 pounds. He was possessed of "prodigious speed,"[2] His dam's sire is also the sire of the dam of Three Bars of Quarter Horse renown. Whatitold You (*Flushing II-St. Elisa by Hadagal) a stakes placed winner of over $98,000 was an even 17:2 while Derby John (John's Joy-Merry Onig by Gino) was an imposing 18 hands.

In modern times, 17:1 hand Forego (*Forli-Lady Golconda by Hasty Road) was winner of Horse of the Year honors. The durable gelding dominated the handicap division, winning all the important races usually under top weight, including the Brooklyn, Suburban, Metropolitan, Woodward, Marlboro Cup and Jockey Club Gold Cup. Risen Star, winner of the Preakness and Belmont in 1988, is 17 hands.

The horse's disposition is an important factor to consider; if it is not good, other considerations such as age, health, sex and soundness are purely academic. It is not advisable to attempt to reschool an ill-tempered or thoroughly spoiled horse. But what can you tell about a horse when he is being kept in an artificial environment such as a training barn at a racetrack? You can observe how he relates to all the activity going on around him. Is he standing, relaxed and eating his hay or is he pinning his ears and biting at everyone within reach? The eye and its expression can tell a lot about the horse's intelligence and temperament. He should appear to be alert, friendly and curious with ears forward. A large, prominent eye is considered to be a kind eye and also a sign of intelligence. Observe his attitude toward his handlers and, most especially, their attitude toward him. Do they observe any particular precautions in handling him? Do they look as if they expect him to bite, kick, or strike? A horse that is racing fit is very sharp and keyed up, so the chain over the nose is routine.

A quick way to get an overall sample of his manners and attitude is to pick out all his feet. If he is cooperative about this aspect of his daily routine, he will, in all likelihood, be cooperative about other things. At the racetrack, all the feet

---

[1] Rhonda Williams, *The Blood-Horse*, telephone conversation, May 1990.
[2] John Hervey, *Racing In America 1922-1936*, (New York: The Jockey Club, 1937), p. 248.

are picked up from the near side, or the horse's left side. The good natured, well mannered horse will lift each foot on command, holding it steady until it is set down. He will shift his weight or even lift the next foot to have it ready for you. Any attempt at resistance, such as putting more weight on the foot you are trying to pick up, snatching the foot away, pawing, striking, nipping, cow kicking or excessive tail switching should be discriminated against.

The perfect horse does not exist. There is no animal that cannot be faulted on one count or another by a discerning eye. Sometimes it takes a better eye to see the good points than to pick out the more obvious defects. The ideal, or absolute, however, should be kept in mind as a standard against which to judge any animal being considered for purchase.

Wins Grand Prix Despite Bowed Tendon

Terry Brown of Canton, Georgia, purchased the former race horse, Misty-Eyed Scholar (One Scholar-Misty Look by Misty Flight) in December of 1982, after the gelding's career ending bowed tendon was well set. After 27 starts in three years of racing, 8 wins, 5 times second and 4 times third, he had earned $41,763. The seven-year-old was renamed Cure the Blues; he has enjoyed great success as a jumper, having earned over $40,000, including the 1989 City Glass Specialty Grand Prix with a $15,000 purse. Cure the Blues is owned by Showcase Ltd. and has been ridden throughout his jumping career by Terry Brown.[3] (Photo courtesy of Pennington Galleries).

---

[3] Terry Brown, Canton, Georgia, letter, May 1990

Chapter 5

Age, Experience & Sex

In selecting a candidate for reschooling, age is an important factor to consider.

Very young horses are seldom available. Trainers are reluctant to pronounce a two-year old hopeless, but will continue to make excuses for him, hoping he will mature into a useful performer. Perhaps "the cough" has set him back or maybe he bucked shins or fell victim to any of the innumerable, and often temporary ills to which the immature horse is liable when subjected to stress.

At two, the Thoroughbred is too young for demanding reschooling. He is two years away from the ideal age to start over fences. However, he can learn the preliminary suppling exercises and can hack out on the trail, building muscle as a foundation for later, serious work while developing calmness and confidence - the much valued "sane mind."

On the other hand many old campaigners have become too confirmed in their habits to make a satisfactory adjustment to another mode of life. Additionally, wear and tear on joints and ligaments increase with continued use. The years of pounding over hard dirt tracks exact their price. Joints (articular surfaces) become arthritic. Tendons and ligaments become less elastic, less resilient.

Although the older racehorse is often a poor risk for reschooling due to his questionable soundness and the fact that his reactions and habitual patterns of behavior have become thoroughly established, many older horses have made excellent

The legendary Kelso shown winning the Suburban at Aqueduct and, in his later years, schooling for an exhibition at Saratoga, trainer Allison Cramm, up. (Photo courtesy The Blood-Horse).

career changes. The durable chestnut gelding Standoff (Broke Even- Steady On by Mate) was foaled in 1948; he broke his maiden at Hialeah as a two-year-old, raced for 9 seasons, until he was ten. Starting 161 times, he won 23 races, was 18 times second and 19 times third. After his retirement he was used as a western pleasure horse for at least another eight years. Three Grand (Condiment-Grand Matron by Johnstown) also had an extended racing career. He started 109 times, winning 15, placing second 15 times and third on 7 occasions. His generous, easy going nature and cheerful outlook on life helped make his transition from track to hack an easy one. He was used as a Pony Club mount for a young girl.

The most distinguished older racehorse to find a new life after the track was Kelso (Your Host-Maid of Flight by Count Fleet), foaled in 1957. He was voted Horse of the Year for an unprecedented five consecutive seasons. He won at distances from 6 furlongs to two miles carrying as much as 136 pounds and conceding weight to his rivals. He broke or equalled 14 track records. He raced for 7 seasons, from 2 through 8. In 63 starts he accounted for 39 wins, was 12 times second and twice third for record earnings of $1,977,896. A record which endured for 15 years, until broken by Triple Crown winner Affirmed in 1979.[1] Five times he won the demanding Jockey Club Gold Cup at two miles. His standard starts index was 110.41 which means that he earned one hundred and ten times more than the average horse of his generation. After his retirement, he was ridden for pleasure by his owner and breeder Mrs. Richard C. duPont. He also carried his mistress to hounds and appeared regularly in dressage exhibitions to raise money for the Grayson Foundation which conducts equine research.

As a general rule, however, the three-year-old or four-year-old maiden, or non-winner, is a preferable choice even to the moderately successful older horse. In the first place, he is more likely to be available than is the successful campaigner. At most tracks, maidens over the age of four are not permitted to race

---

[1] Rhonda Williams, Editorial Department, *The Blood-Horse*, telephone communication, 1990.

or to be stabled on the grounds. Nowhere do trainers have an easy time obtaining stall space for them.

The maiden is less likely to be for sale due to a soundness problem than is the old campaigner with many hard miles on him. Just as most of us would prefer to buy the cream puff used car driven by the mythical little old lady than the car used as a taxi, so it is preferable to buy the maiden who suffered lack of aggressiveness or speed (measured in fractions of seconds) than the older horse. There is an old saying that some horses have never run fast enough to hurt themselves.

Because horsemen are eternally optimistic (otherwise they would all be doing something else for a living) mares, even those with dismal race records and undistinguished lineage, are thought to be capable of being producers of winners, or with a little luck, "a real good one." Surprisingly, upon occasion they do just that. Carry Back, winner of the Kentucky Derby, Preakness and many other important stakes was produced by Joppy, a non-winner, whose first and second dams also failed to ever get home in front. Or, consider Hildene, earner of a grand total of $100 at the races, who produced the stakes winners Hill Prince, Prince Hill, First Landing, Third Brother, Mangohick and winner Satsuma, the dam of champion Cicada the leading money winning filly of her era with lifetime earnings of $783,674. Mares, therefore, are not as readily sold at pleasure horse prices as are geldings.

Many colts and entire horses, whose racetrack performance or pedigree do not warrant a chance at stud are available at bargain prices. Unless they are first gelded, they are not good candidates for reschooling.

An ungelded colt is often difficult to handle, biting being only one of the undesirable behavior traits of an entire male horse. Rather than responding to your wishes, he is controlled by the unruly dictates of his hormones. His sensitive sense of smell can detect a mare in heat at distances up to half a mile. His mind and whole being will respond to the siren song of pheromones, rather than to what you may be trying to persuade him to do. He is literally incapable of paying attention. While it is true that it is possible to train a colt or a horse to go quietly in company and to deny his instincts in the show ring, few riders have the skill and patience to accomplish this goal. At the racetrack, colts and entire horses have, of necessity, been in close association with fillies and mares, being stabled in the same barns and run in the same races. Evidences of studdiness have been quickly and firmly censured, often to such a degree that when retired to the breeding shed, the prospective stallion will be shy about displaying libido, since he has been taught that such behavior was unacceptable and reprehensible. Stallions are prohibited by A.H.S.A. rules from participating in classes restricted to lady and junior riders. Nowhere are they welcome. Many public stables discriminate against them by refusing to accept them as boarders, or by charging a premium for their care. Because the incentive to get loose is greater in entire horses, they are notorious escape artists. You, the owner, are legally responsible for whatever damage he does.

So if the horse you select and must have is a colt, have him gelded. One benefit of gelding a horse after he matures is that he will have a prettier head and a better developed neck and front than a gelding altered early in life. Castration is a minor surgical procedure. You can arrange to have it done by one of the veterinarians at the racetrack before you bring him home or by an equine practitioner at your own barn.

After surgery, a day's stall rest in a large stall deeply bedded with straw is followed with hand walking 20 minutes twice a day. As an alternative, the gelding can be turned out in a small, grassy paddock where he can be observed to make certain that he takes enough exercise to minimize swelling. Chase him around the paddock, if necessary, or longe him several times a day for a few minutes. Some swelling is normal. Due to swelling, the empty scrotum will look like the testes are still in place for a few days following surgery. His hind legs and scrotal area can be cold hosed daily to reduce swelling and to clean off the blood and fluids which drain from the incisions. Dribbling blood is normal following surgery, spurting blood is not. Phone your veterinarian immediately if you observe more than a faint trickle of blood. Check on him during the night to make sure he is still all right. A horse can bleed to death following castration, so be alert and don't let it happen to you.

Due to the inevitable drainage, a colt should not be castrated in fly season. Under normal circumstances, the new gelding will have made a full recovery in a week to ten days. It will take from six months to a year for the testosterone circulating in his bloodstream to dissipate. He may remain "studdy" in his behavior upon occasion for the rest of his life.

Track Campaigner Likes Pony Clubbing

Crazy William (Beach City-Dear Allis by All Hands) a dark bay or brown gelding, foaled in 1972 was campaigned hard for eight seasons, making 112 starts of which he won 13, placing second 16 times and third 12 times for earnings of $34,394. He was bought by Anne Parish of Cataula, Georgia, for her daughter to event and show. He was renamed Double Shadow. The pair, always in the ribbons, moved up through Novice, Training and Preliminary Levels and earned the B Pony Club rating. They do both dressage and jumper classes. Double Shadow is described as a bold jumper, honest, elegant and very athletic. At 18 years, he looks more like a four-year-old than his actual years. (Photo courtesy of Anne Parrish).

Chapter 6

Picking Your Favorite Color

There is a saying that good horses come in all colors, and that a good horse was never a bad color. Many horsemen have strong preferences, prejudices and opinions concerning color, but fortunately they are unable to agree and we continue to have variety.

In some breeds of horses used for show, flashy, eye catching coloration wins prominence. For example, chestnut is the favored and predominant color for American Saddle Horses. One talented, big going, gray fine harness mare failed to win a ribbon until her owner *dyed* her a flaming chestnut and renamed her Painted Lady. After that, she won everything in sight - but that's another story!

The Thoroughbred, however, never has been a breed where coat color was given much consideration. Appearance has always been of secondary importance to racetrack performance. There have been times when certain coat colors have been favored or discriminated against but such preference has always been based on practical considerations or upon the mistaken belief that the favored color resulted in better performance.

Of the original foundation sires, the Darley Arabian was bay, the Godolphin Arabian was dappled bay-brown and the Byerly Turk was brown.

Bay is by far the most common coat color comprising 43 per cent of the total registry. Bay was the favored color at one time because it was the color of the largest number of stakes winners. But the percentage of bay stakes winners was shown to be identical to the percentage of bay Thoroughbreds registered. Many horsemen prefer a deep bay to a light one, believing that washy colors are a sign of weakness. The brilliant champion filly La Prevoyante's performance refutes the above prejudice. A 1970 daughter of champion Buckpasser out of Arctic Dancer (Nearctic-Natalma by Native Dancer), a full sister to Northern Dancer, La Prevoyante won 25 of 39 starts, earning $572,417 and honors as champion 2-year old filly in the United States and Horse of the Year in Canada. She was such a light bay that she might have been described as "buckskin" in another stud book - the color of light tan craft paper - the "plain brown wrapper."

Another common coat color in the Thoroughbred is brown, a deep walnut or ebony hue, distinguishable from black at certain times of the year only by the presence of tan hairs on the muzzle and flanks. The "dark colors" which include bay, brown and black total 64 per cent of the registry.

Chestnut, the most eye catching color, is said to go with a fiery temperament. This belief may be more than mere superstition, and there well may be a positive correlation between coat color and temperament. Both hair and nervous tissue derive from the same primitive germ cell layer, the ectoderm.[1] Although chestnut (which is expressed as the absence of the patterning factor which causes black points (mane, tail, legs and sometimes muzzle and ear tips) may range from light yellow-gold, through ginger to liver that verges on black, the most common tint among Thoroughbreds is red chestnut; in fact, "Big Red" was the nickname applied to Man O'War and in a later generation, Secretariat. Usually a chestnut horse's mane and tail are the same color as his body, but occasionally, they are distinctly lighter or darker. In North America, 30 per cent of all Thoroughbreds are registered as chestnut.

Gray is an impermanent color. At birth the foal is black, brown or chestnut. The clue that he will change color is his

---

[1] Leslie Brainerd Arey, Ph.D., Sc.D., L.L.D. *Developmental Anatomy*, (Philadelphia, Pa.: W. B. Saunders Company, 1941.)

darker than normal foal coat. Also, to be gray, he must have at least one gray parent. When the baby hair begins to shed, a few white hairs can be seen around the eyes and muzzle and also high on the poll behind the ears. With each change of coat the number of white hairs increases while the pigmented hairs become darker and the horse successively goes through the stages of iron gray, dappled gray, flea bitten gray, until in old age he is pure white. Roan, which genetically is the same trait as gray, is a mixture of reddish, rather than dark hairs, with white. Many bizarre patterns and colors have been classified as roan, including the white colt foaled at Patchen Wilkes Farm near Lexington, Kentucky, named War Colors. He had a jaunty chestnut poll cap and chestnut ears.

A distinct disadvantage of gray horses is their tendency to develop melanomas (darkly pigmented tumors, literally, "black") on the hairless areas of their bodies, particularly around the dock, anus, genitalia and also, less commonly, on the eyelids, lips and nostrils. Occasionally melanomas grow on the inner lining of the mouth where they can interfere with chewing. Although they are usually benign, equine melanomas may become malignant, therefore, on average, a gray Thoroughbred's life expectancy is slightly shorter than that of his dark or chestnut relatives. By the time they reach the age of 15, 80% of all gray or roan horses will have developed melanomas. While these lesions remain benign for an average of 10 or 15 years, malignant cases which spread to the internal organs are rapidly fatal.[2]

The gray or roan coat color fell into disfavor in England for many years. Except for ceremonial purposes, grays were discriminated against by the military because they offered a too attractive and easily visible target to the enemy.

In former times grays were considered to have early speed but to be without heart or bottom. Beautiful gray *Mahmoud (*Blenheim II-Mah Mahal by Gainsborough) destroyed that prejudice by the definitive way in which he won the mile and one half Derby at Epsom in 1936, setting a new course record.

---

[2] P. W. Pratt, MVD, editor, *Equine Medicine and Surgery*, American Veterinary Publications, Santa Barbara, California, 1982, Vol II, p. 808.

The number of grays increased from a very rare color to 6 per cent of the total registry, partly due to the popularity of *Mahmoud and his progeny and their successes on the track and in the stud.

Black is a rare color.

There are no pinto or spotted Thoroughbreds, but natural white markings other than on the face or legs occur occasionally. They are not discriminated against by the American Stud Book as they are in several other North American light horse registries which are concerned more with appearance than performance.

Some Thoroughbreds have a sprinkling of white hairs throughout their coats, especially in the flanks and at the root of the tail. This characteristic is referred to as "Birdcatcher ticking" in deference to an early stallion with white hairs sprinkled throughout his bay coat.

White markings vary from splashy to nonexistent. There is almost always some white on the face, even if it is only a few scattered hairs, most often in the whorl or cowlick between the eyes. White socks and feet are not quite so common as they are in other breeds where "lots of chrome" may be sought after. Many Thoroughbred horsemen dislike white feet because the non-pigmented horn extruded from the white coronary areas is thought to lack the strength and vitality of pigmented hoof; thus the adage warning that a horse with four white feet is fit only to feed to the crows.

COWLICK GUIDE

Ⓐ BEHIND POLL
Ⓑ HIGH AT CREST OF NECK
Ⓒ MIDDLE OF CREST OF NECK
Ⓓ LOW AT CREST OF NECK
Ⓔ JUGULAR GROOVE

FOREHEAD
EYE LEVEL
CENTER OF FACE
BRIDGE OF NOSE

Cowlick to left above
eye level.

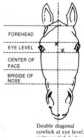

FOREHEAD
EYE LEVEL
CENTER OF FACE
BRIDGE OF NOSE

Double diagonal
cowlick at eye level,
right cowlick higher.

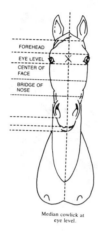

FOREHEAD
EYE LEVEL
CENTER OF FACE
BRIDGE OF NOSE

Median cowlick at
eye level.

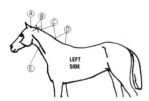

B) Cowlick high at crest of neck.

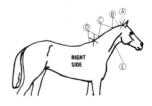

A) Cowlick behind poll.
D) Cowlick low at crest of neck.

The location of cowlicks aid in the identification of Thoroughbreds.
(Courtesy of The Jockey Club)

Reschooled for Dressage

In 18 starts in two seasons, By Birth (Mac Diamida-Birthday Witch by Hoist the Flag), a 15:2 hand bay gelding foaled in 1983, a half-brother to multiple stakes winner, Bold Spectacle ($149,249), was once second and once third for earnings of $3,771. He was purchased for $200 from a Florida horse dealer by Elly Schobel as a "skinny, unsound ex-race horse". As a dressage horse, his achievements have been of quite a different order. Starting in First Level in the 1989-90 winter season, he rapidly advanced to Third Level and Fourth Level. He was consistently in the top three which is "even more remarkable considering the tough warmblood competition he had to face each time out and the large classes on the Florida circuit." Elly has progressed to Prix St. Georges with him since this photo was taken and will continue on in FEI in the comming years, stating that he already shows remarkable skill and talent for piaffe and flying changes.[3] (Photo courtesy of Terri Miller).

---

[3] Elly Schobel, Palm City Florida, Letter, May 1990

Chapter 7

How to Spot Unsoundness

Thoroughbreds begin training at a very early age and because of the extreme stress of racing, the incidence of unsoundness is high. As in conformation, an absolute in soundness is something which does not exist. This is true not only of the Throughbred but all other breeds of horses as well. There are certain defects with which a horse can perform more or less efficiently. Other ailments are far more serious and sharply curtail his usefulness. There are thousands of horses that cannot withstand the strain of hard race training, but can do admirably at less demanding tasks.

When examining your reschooling prospect, one of your primary concerns will be to determine whether he is lame or sound. Because the forelegs bear the greater portion of the horse's weight (60%), they are far more likely to become unsound than are the hind limbs, which have their own specific problems. The cause of 90% of lameness is in the foot. Of the remaining 10%, 90% is at or below the fetlock, while the balance, only 1%, is at, or below, the knee and hock. Therefore, the hip and shoulder are less probable sites of trouble.

In checking for lameness, observe the horse first at a walk and then at the trot. Deficiencies in way of going are more obvious when the horse is observed from behind. A free moving horse with a big stride will swing the hind legs well under himself at the walk, overstepping the track of the front hoof by as much as a foot. Any defect of gait is far more apparent at the trot than at the walk. If the horse is off in one foreleg, he will nod his head as the opposite foreleg strikes the ground and assumes more of the horse's weight.

Hind limb lameness is more difficult to locate. Often it seems that the horse is lame in the opposite foreleg. To identify hock lameness, hold the leg in a flexed position for two or three minutes; then have him trotted briskly. The flexion test will exaggerate any fault in his gait, making it more readily apparent, perhaps confirming what you thought you saw. Have the horse turned sharply. If he is sore in any joint, he will pivot around it, rather than flexing the joint.

The horse which is lame in all four legs may appear to go sound, since he does not favor one leg more than another, but it is usually possible to detect an overall stiffness and a reluctance to move out.

The traditional methods of treating lameness in horses are blistering and firing, forms of counter-irritation. Counter-irritation endures despite the development of non-steroidal anti-inflammatory medications (NSAI), whirlpool massage machines, DMSO, poultices and liniments. The theory of counter-irritation is to convert a chronic or low level inflammation to an acute, active inflammatory process in order that it may be more quickly resolved. Since counter-irritation increases the inflammation which, in turn, increases the blood supply to the affected area, it is believed this will remove the debris and sources of pain. In reality, rest from training which the fired or blistered horse must, of necessity receive, is a major part of the success of the treatment.

Blistering is induced by the application of a caustic agent such as croton oil, strong iodine, muriatic acid, cantharides or iodide of mercury. In addition to commercial preparations each stable has its own favorite recipe that promises near magic results. The degree of irritation caused varies with the strength of the caustic agent, the individual horse's sensitivity and whether the legs are bandaged or left open. Bandaging increases the severity of the blister, as does using a layer of plastic wrap under the bandage to trap the generated heat. Thin skinned, light colored horses are more likely to experience a severe reaction than are thick skinned, dark legged horses. White legs are particularly vulnerable. Before application of the blister, the legs are clipped, then washed with soap and water to remove the natural protective oils from the skin. As the counter-irritant takes effect, blisters form, the legs swell and serum oozes out. As the wet, or acute phase passes, swelling and heat subside. The legs dry, the superficial layers of skin scurf and slough off. New hair and skin are formed. In a month or more, the leg will return to its former appearance, although various lumps and swellings may have disappeared, having been resorbed during the inflammatory process.

During the acute phase of the blister the horse must wear a cradle to keep him from trying to bite or rub the affected area. Sometimes horses chew away skin, tendon and bone in an attempt to alleviate the pain and subsequent itching. If the blistering agent gets in the horse's eyes, as it surely will if he is allowed to rub his face on his legs, the corneas will ulcerate causing permanent scarring or blindness.

Firing is a more drastic means of inducing counter-irritation. Therapeutic cautery, as it is called, leaves a permanent reminder of the injury or unsoundness which it purports to treat. In many instances, firing is a mutilating operation which compounds the problem, rather than effecting a cure. The firing iron, heated to a cherry-red heat, is jabbed into the anesthetized leg at intervals of not less than 3/8 of an inch. The depth of penetration may vary from a mere pricking of the skin to a deep, bone searing pit. Fortunately, firing is not employed as much today as it was in the past, due to the development and use of non-steroidal anti-inflammatory agents such as Phenylbutazone (bute), Banamine and Azium.

As the lesions caused by firing heal, they leave small scars which look like dots set in a geometric pattern. If the firing was severe, the hair follicles are destroyed and thus the scarring will be very distinct. Sometimes the hair follicles may have been damaged, in which case the hair will grow back white. In milder cases, the pattern is so faint that it can be seen only in an oblique light where it looks like a design on watered silk.

If a horse suits you in all other respects, I would not be put off by the presence of scars from pinfiring. It used to be a standard treatment for bucked shins, an affliction that 70%[1] of all two-year-olds in race training experience. If the horse returned to racing soundness after having been fired, chances are he will stand up to whatever you wish to do with him. The forelegs of the gelding Nichols W. (Marcador-Woodbreak by *Unbreakable) bore the scars of the firing iron on shins and ankles. I rode him for twenty years, occasionally as much as thirty miles in a day. He was still sound at his death at the age of twenty-five, although he was never pampered in any way. His legs were never done up except when he was recovering from being hit by a car. Although the horse completely overcame his rather severe injuries, the car was a total wreck.

Firing Leaves Geometric Scars

[1] P.W. Prat ed. *Op. Cit.* p. 1110

There are a number of common injuries and conditions which you are likely to come across in your search for a reschooling prospect. While these conditions are not unique to racehorses, they perhaps are seen more frequently in racehorses than in horses engaged in other activities. Listed below are some of the most common conditions and how each affects reschooling.

Osselets: One of the most common defects found in racehorses is the formation of osselets, a deposit of calcium on the fetlock or ankle. Osselets vary in size from a slight thickening of the fetlock to a grossly distorted joint twice the normal size. It is difficult to judge the degree of gait impairment from the external appearance.

The parts of the joints which turn on each other are called the articular surfaces. Bone is covered with smooth, white, glistening articular cartilage which is lubricated with synovial fluid. A normal joint functions smoothly. Under hard use, the articular cartilages may become worn and pitted with irregular rather than smooth surfaces; tearing of the joint capsule allows the synovial fluid to leak. New bone may be deposited on the articular surfaces (intra-articular) or on another portion of the joint (extra-articular). Intra-articular exostosis (deposit of new bone) is a painful and very serious condition, while extra-articular exostosis, while unsightly, is benign unless it interferes with a tendon or ligament. X-ray or ultrasound examination can determine the extent and location of new bone formation.

An osselet begins as a soft swelling with heat. Lameness or reluctance to move forward may be present in varying degree. Gradually, as the joint capsule degenerates, leakage of synovial fluid occurs due to tearing of the joint capsule. Later, new bone is laid down in the affected area - the body's attempt to reinforce a damaged structure. X-ray examination will show the formation of new bone.

If the exostosis (deposit of new bone) invades the articular surface of the joint, lameness will be severe and the prognosis is grave. Although the lameness is pronounced when osselets are "green," they may cause very little problem when they are "set" or "cold." The body has great recuperative powers, remodeling itself to adapt to stress and injury.

If you like the horse and he jogs sound, I would not hesitate to buy him despite the osselet. For your peace of mind, have a few X-rays taken. The gelding Creche (Bimelech-Rockabye by *Blenheim II) had an enormous osselet when we bought him at six. We got him started over fences and sold him to Roger Boltz of Bath, Ohio, who rode him in Pony Club, hunted him for many seasons and showed him extensively over a long period of time, during which the horse remained sound.

Bucked Shins: Another stress induced affliction, especially common among two-year olds, is the condition known as bucked shins. Bone is living, dynamic tissue, constantly being laid down and resorbed to be shaped into new configuration in response to the demands made upon it. As the cannon bones are remodeled from round to ovoid (on cross section) to better support the stresses of training, a vascular lattice work of new bone tissue is laid down along the front of the bones. This new tissue is fragile, thus easily damaged by the concussion of hitting a hard surface at speed. Minute fractures occur, accompanied by bleeding, inflammation, acute pain and lameness. As seen from the side, there is an outward bulging of the cannon bones.

Although the lameness from bucked shins is acute, it is temporary. The condition yields to rest followed by a more conservative work load. As in most cases, the body heals itself. There is no residual unsoundness from bucked shins.

Ringbone: Ringbone is a bony growth often accompanied by erosion of the joints below the fetlock. The condition causes lameness at the time the new bone is being laid down. Whether the lameness is permanent depends upon the location of the bony growth.

There will not be lasting disability unless it is located in a position to irritate the common extensor tendon or unless the articular surfaces are involved. The gross appearance is essentially the same - a bulging outward at the coronet (low ringbone) or at the dorsal surface of the pastern (high ringbone). Because of the difficulty in distinguishing between true (articular) ringbone, a grave unsoundness, and so-called false ringbone (ringbone that does not involve the joint and which causes lameness only when "green"), it is best to avoid horses with bony outgrowths on the coronet and pastern, unless they can be X-rayed or examined by ultrasound scan and declared to be a reasonable risk for your purpose.

Suspensory Ligament and Sesamoid Problems: Suspensory ligament and sesamoid bone problems seem to run hand-in-hand. The suspensory ligament branches at the back of the fetlock and passes over the two sesamoid bones which are pyramidal in shape. Injury to the ligaments at the point where they are attached to the sesamoids causes inflammation to both of the small bones and to the tendon sheath. The sesamoids become inflamed and decalcified. The back of the fetlock looks swollen and it feels hot to the touch. There will be a choppiness of the horse's gait when he gallops over a hard surface, although he may appear to move more normally over a soft or yielding surface. If the tendon shortens due to the inflammatory process, the fetlock will have a tendency to knuckle over and the horse will stumble.

A horse with suspensory ligament damage often has degenerating sesamoids and is a poor risk for strenuous use. Fracture of the sesamoids with rupture of the suspensory ligaments is one of the most common career and life ending racetrack injuries. There always exists the risk of this major injury in jumping or in the upper levels of eventing particularly when the integrety of the suspensory ligaments and sesamoids is already compromised. Olympic gold medal winner, Jim Day of Canada, "is . . . not very keen on sesamoid problems for a horse destined to become a jumper, although he finds them acceptable for a hunter."[2]

Due to the erosion of the sesamoid bones as they degenerate, they become liable to fracture, especially when fatigue is very great and the fetlock joint is overextended so that the back of the pastern actually strikes the ground. The toe grab on racing

---

[2] Rita M. Jefferies, *loc.cit.*

plates has the effect of lengthening the toe, increasing the likelihood of overextension.

Fracture of the sesamoids is a very grave injury from which few horses recover. Horses with fractured sesamoids can sometimes be saved for breeding, but they have little other future. Be suspicious of any horse with a tender swelling or thickening at the back of the fetlock. While certain individuals with inflamed sesamoid bones can be used for light riding after a period of rest, jumping or fast work should be avoided.

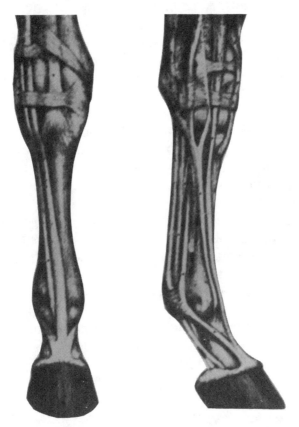

Diagram Showing How Suspensory Ligaments and Sesamoid Bones Are Tied Together.
(Drawing courtesy of Ray Antoniowicz, University of Wisconsin)

Bowed Tendons: Bowed tendons are a common injury. The condition may vary in degree from a slight strain, to an actual rupture of the bundles of fibers that make up the tendon. Depending upon the severity, there is more or less heat, swelling, bleeding and seeping of serum into the surrounding areas. After the acute stage passes, heat and swelling subside but a thickening and bowing backward of the tendon will remain. The injury is repaired by the formation of scar tissue. These adhesions result in loss of elasticity and diminished function. The area will be subject to future injury. In some horses, the bowed look is not evident on visual examination, but a thickened area along the back of the tendon can be felt. An ultrasound scan is helpful in assessing the degree of injury.

With a year's rest at pasture, training can be resumed. Many horses return to racing, but at a lower level of competition, provided that the original injury was not too severe.

Splints: To understand splints, one must first understand the anatomy of horses' legs. Although splints can occur in any leg, the front legs which carry more than their share of the burden (60%) are most commonly afflicted. Through the ages, the horse evolved from a three-toed animal. The splint bones (small metacarpal bones) lie on either side of the cannon bones. They are vestiges (remnants) of prehistoric toes. Proof of this fact is that on rare occasions when splint bones grow abnormally long, there will be a tiny hoof at the bottom (distal) end, like a dog's dew claw. Splint bones narrow to mere slivers of bone at their lower end. They are described as being incomplete because they do not extend to the bottom of the cannon bone. At their tops, the splint bones articulate with the lower row of carpal bones, forming part of the carpometacarpal joint, the lowest of the three joints which comprise the knee. The splint bones are bound to the cannon by an interosseus ligament. Because the splint bones are incomplete, there is some movement in them. Being part of the knee joint, they are also weight bearing. Excessive motion, such as is generated by pounding on a hard racetrack at speed, or rapid changes of direction, throws excessive stress on the interosseus ligament which becomes irritated and inflamed. New bone is deposited in the inflamed area. In the mature horse, the splint bones become fused to the cannon in their upper portion; the ligament is converted to bone. Thus horses do not usually develop splints when they are over the age of six.

Splints may vary in size from a tiny irregularity which can be felt rather than seen to an unsightly lump the size of a hen's egg. Splints, like many other conditions involving new growth of bone, are painful when they are developing, but constitute a blemish, rather than an unsoundness when cooled out and set, unless they are located so close to the knee as to interfere with its function.

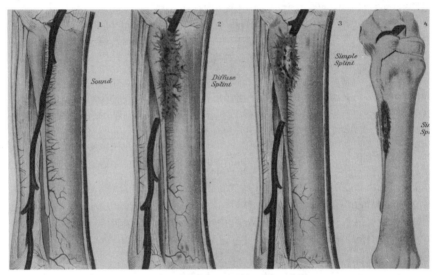

Diagram showing splint location

Knee Injuries: The knee is actually made up of three joints: the radiocarpal joint, the middle carpal joint and the carpometacarpal joint. There are at least seven, sometimes eight small bones in two rows, bound together by ligaments. Damage to the knee is most frequently caused by over-extension. In addition to over-extension, the knee can be damaged by concussion, by twisting and by falls and kicks. It is difficult to predict how knee injuries will affect a horse's future soundness. Horses vary in their recuperative power and in their tolerance to pain. If the horse is able to race after a knee injury, he can, most likely, hold up to whatever you wish to use him for, provided you exercise reasonable care in warming him up and in cooling him out, using bandages and liniment, cold hosing and NSAI medication as recommended by your veterinarian. Horses with horrible looking knees may still perform well.

In checking for knee damage, flex the leg so that the heel of the foot touches the horse's elbow, a motion which the normal knee performs easily. Inability to flex the knee fully is a sign of pain. Because of the difficulty in flexing the knee, a horse with knee lameness will walk with a paddling motion, swinging the affected leg outward, avoiding bending it as much as possible. As in any other type of joint problem, the difference between use and unsoundness is the location of the new bone - articular or extrarticular - something that cannot be told for certain without a set of X-rays or an ultrasound scan. Knees are not easy to bandage; in order to keep a knee wrap from slipping, the bandage is sometimes applied so tightly that the hair follicles on the back of the knee over the accessory carpal bone are damaged, leaving a tell-tale patch of white hairs - a warning flag that the horse has had a problem with his knees, which otherwise might appear to be unblemished.

In the rear leg of young horses, the knee cap (patella) may have a tendency to slip. The tendency is more marked in cowhocked horses. Usually the weakness is corrected by exercise. As the horse's muscular strength increases, the ligaments and tendons which support the patella also become stronger. The stifle joint (which the patella protects) itself may be the site of arthritic changes that cause dragging or scuffing of the toe of the affected leg. The horse will "tight rope" walk due to limitations of motion in the joint; he will swing the leg so that the hind foot touches the ground behind the opposite foreleg.

Fractures of the Small Bones in the Foot: Fracture of any of the small bones of the foot causes lameness, heat and pain. The horse usually points the affected foot, resting it to alleviate its discomfort. Olympian Jim Day avoids horses with broken bones in their feet, never having had much luck dealing with foot problems, which he finds rarely heal properly.[3]

Spavins: Afflictions of the hocks are called spavins. Jacks are bony out-growths of the hock; they may or may not cause lameness. Bog spavins are soft swellings, a result of excess accumulation of synovial fluid in one of the bursal sacks. Bog spavins are most often seen in young horses who have been stressed; they are more of a cosmetic than a functional problem and usually improve as the animal matures.[4]

A toe-stabbing gait is typical of a horse with a bone spavin, a much more serious affliction. Eventually the intertarsal joints fuse, a process which takes several months. Although the lameness will be lessened, there will also be restricted motion of the hock. The outlook is not good, although some horses with mild cases respond favorably to NSAI therapy.

Capped Elbows (Shoe Boils): Bursal enlargements of the elbow joint are called capped elbows or shoe boils. Pressure of the shod forefoot pressing against the horse's elbow when he lies down, causes irritation and swelling of the skin and tissue. Certain horses with extremely high action may actually strike their elbow when galloping. Continued irritation is prevented by the horse's wearing a shoe boil boot - a padded leather doughnut-shaped pad - around his pastern when he is in his stall, to prevent the shoe resting against the elbow when the horse lies down. There will be a more or less permanent bursal swelling, comparable to the residual enlargement of capped hocks.

Capped Hocks: Capped hocks are enlargements of the sacs (bursa) containing lubricating fluids at the back of the joint. These bursal enlargements are caused by direct trauma, most likely from the horse kicking the wall of the stall, or from being knocked about in a rough trailer or van ride. Capped hocks are

---

[3] Rita M. Jefferies, *loc. cit.*
[4] P. W. Pratt, VMP, ed., *Equine Medicine and Surgery,* Vol II, American Veterinary Publications, Santa Barbara, CA., 1982, p. 1142.

considered to be a blemish, rather than an unsoundness. After the swelling subsides, the hocks will never quite return to their previous size; they are subject to recurring irritation because, now being more prominent, they are more subject to re-injury. The horse that once capped his hocks kicking the wall is likely to do so again.

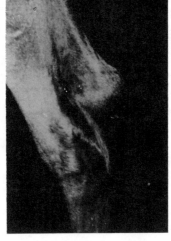

Capped Hocks Are Considered a Blemish, Not Unsoundness
(Photo courtesy of Ray Antoniowicz, University of Wisconsin)

Nerving: Sometimes, the posterior digital nerve of the horse is intentionally severed which desensitizes the foot. This procedure is performed to relieve severe pain - pain which does not respond to more conservative treatment. Although it enables a horse to train and to race, it does nothing to alleviate the underlying condition which is the cause of pain. It is difficult to make a guess as to the horse's future soundness if the condition for which he was nerved in unknown. A series of foot X-rays or scans will probably answer that question. In buying a horse for resale, you should know that many veterinarians will not pass a nerved horse no matter how sound he is clinically. The foot of a nerved horse tends to degenerate due to accidental injury because bruises and subsolar abscesses, if they occur, cause no pain until it is too late to treat them properly. A list of nerved horses is usually posted in the racing secretary's office. Volar neurotomy (high nerving) is seldom performed since the blood supply to the foot is compromised and the hoof will fall off. High nerved horses are barred from racing in all racing jurisdictions.

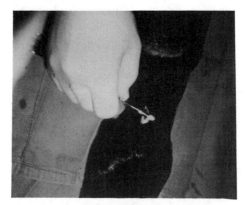

Severing the Nerve Desensitizes the Foot
(Photo courtesy of Ray Antoniowicz, University of Wisconsin)

Back Injuries: Injury to the lumbar vertebrae which are the last bones in the body to calcify completely cause vague, intermittent hind end lameness which is very difficult to pin point or to diagnose.

Some strained muscles in the hind quarters respond to rest; others do not. A spur of bone may impinge upon a nerve causing pain or loss of function. Some horses respond to NSAI agents while others remain "cold backed." Certain horses will flinch when you touch or press down on the muscles of their backs, while others do not react until the full weight of the rider is in the saddle. The may crouch and hunch down when first mounted, or may respond with a vigorous buck or series of bucks to the stimulus of back pain. Some horses move off stiffly when first mounted and then warm out of it to move normally. Because of the equivocal nature of back problems, it is important to have the horse evaluated by a veterinarian specializing in horses who is well aware of the nature of the athletic demands you plan to place upon the horse. Many conditions resolve themselves, while others become progressively more serious.

Eye Problems: Eye injuries are common in racing. Pieces of mud, sand and gravel are thrown into the runners' faces by the hooves of the horses in front of them. A horse with vision in only one eye is permitted to race with the blind eye covered by a closed blinker cup to protect it from the pain of additional injury which would cause the horse to swerve and interfere with another horse. Horses with impaired vision in both eyes are barred from racing. Since there are quite a few one-eyed horses in active training, checking the prospect's eyes should not be overlooked.

A "feather", or small whitish area on the cornea, is a scar from an old injury and unless extensive, should not be discriminated against severely. A blind eye is often milky white over its entire surface, but this is not always so. Often a blind eye tears excessively. After the horse has been blind for a while, the eye atrophies; it shrinks into its socket, appearing distinctly smaller than the normal eye. A one-eyed horse develops the habit of swinging his head far around to look at objects on his blind side with his remaining good eye; the gesture is quite characteristic and unmistakable.

Since the horse has a very narrow field of binocular vision, and since he makes little use of the small amount he has, judging the distance from things by other visual clues, loss of an eye is not as serious a handicap as loss of an eye would be to you. He should have no trouble learning to jump if the obstacles are solid looking and have a good ground line. It is important to ride him with confidence. The one-eyed horse, however, is likely to be startled by anything coming up on him from his blind side. Speak to him in a reassuring manner so he will know you are there. A one-eyed horse will be more likely than a horse with normal vision to bump into door jambs and fences and to crowd or step on his handlers.

If the blind eye is chronically infected, and the infection is resistant to treatment, the eye must be removed since the infection can readily travel up the optic nerve to the point where it crosses with the optic nerve from the opposite eye, then travel down that nerve to infect and destroy the good eye. Sewing shut the lids of the blind eye will protect it from further injury. A horse with impaired vision in both eyes is dangerous because he cannot see where he is going.

Bleeding: If the horse is not sound in wind, as well as eye and limb, he is of limited usefulness. Probably the most common wind problem at the racetrack is bleeding, or exercise induced pulmonary hemorrhage. It was formally believed that the blood which flowed from the affected horse's nostril came from the nasal passages. Better diagnostic methods show that the bleeding actually occurs in the lungs, due, it is postulated, to pulmonary hypertension under extreme stress. Blood is not always visible at the nostrils and can sometimes only be seen by endoscopic examination. Typical of the horse that bleeds is one running well which stops as if he'd run into a wall. When the horse starts to bleed, he chokes, coughs and cannot continue to put out a maximum effort. In all racing jurisdictions except New York, bleeders may race on Lasix (furosemide), a diuretic, the use of which decreases the pressure in the pulmonary artery through reducing the total volume of circulating blood. The use of Lasix is a matter of public record in almost all racing jurisdictions (except New York where its use is prohibited). A list of horses which are bleeders is usually posted in the racing secretary's office and is published in the Daily Racing Form. Endoscopic examination has revealed that as many as 80% of all horses racing suffer from exercise induced pulmonary hemorrhage.

Since your horse's work/stress level will not approach racing, the fact that he bled at the track should not affect his performance except at the upper levels of eventing.

Roaring: Paralysis of the recurrent laryngeal nerve causes paralysis of the left branch of the larynx, partially obstructing the airway. Reduction in the horse's supply of oxygen causes poor performance, exercise intolerance and "roaring" due to the characteristic sound the horse makes when he works or races. The condition can be alleviated by surgery.

While roarers are suitable for relatively low stress activity, they are not candidates for highly demanding sports such as the upper levels of eventing unless a prosthesis has been surgically inserted to hold back the paralyzed branch of the larynx preventing its obstructing the airway.

Heaves: It is unlikely that you will see a horse at the race track with an advanced case of heaves (aveolar emphysema). A horse suffering from heaves is simply unable to compete athletically due to his compromised intake of oxygen. You may, however, see a former race horse with heaves at a poorly ventilated, damp sales barn where he has been fed musty hay and has stood in a dirty stall inhaling ammonia fumes from urine-soaked bedding.

The horse with heaves or emphysema is not of much use for any purpose. While the condition is not immediately life threatening, the horse will be in distress when exercised and he will have an unthrifty appearance. He will not have trouble inhaling, but must use his abdominal muscles to help expel the air from his damaged lungs. In heaves the alveoli, or airsacks in the lungs, have lost their elasticity due to chronic irritation from inhaling dust or mould in bad hay. The feeding of beet pulp instead of hay has helped many horses with heaves to lead useful lives as pleasure horses.

Colonel William H. Henderson, a prominent horse show judge and a former member of the board of directors of the American Horse Show Association, has the following to say about the blemishes your Thoroughbred hunter prospect has acquired at the racetrack and how they will affect his acceptance in the show ring: "A horse is 'hunting sound' when he has no illness, blemish or conformation fault which would prevent his being able to jog out sound at the completion of his class. . .But bone spavins, bog spavins, side bones and all the many other things which so often afflict the working hunter, do not count against him as long as they are not causing any immediate lameness or unsoundness. Your horse may enter the ring and have as good a chance as the best horse there, despite his bumps and blemishes, if they do not interfere with his performance over fences.[5]"

---

[5] William H. Henderson, in Gordon Wright's *Learning to Ride, Hunt and Show,* Garden City

71

Getting Better at Twenty-Eight

Firm Shock (Ky Colonel-Blueruth by Blue Swords), 1962, winner of 7 races in 54 starts over 5 seasons and $22,865, at twenty-eight years, in owner Anne Wiegle's words"...is now one of my schoolmasters and is used for lessons as a special treat for my very favored students. He does very lovely Third Level work, although we don't work him very hard anymore. He is still sound (no bute!) due to his very correct conformation...Every year we kept thinking that this horse would never last another year, and every year he gets better." Anne Wiegle of Springhill Farm, Pottstown, Pennsylvania, bought Firm Shock when he was nineteen, after a checkered career as failed polo pony, as a preliminary event horse and as a staff horse for Andrews Bridge Hunt. At the age of twenty-two, he was retired from jumping to concentrate on dressage. At twenty-three and twenty-four, he represented the Oley Valley CTA at the Gladstone Team Dressage Competition. He last appeared at a recognized dressage show at the age of 26! Which only demonstrates that with proper care the Thoroughbred is not only a very docile and versatile animal, but also a very durable one. (Photo courtesy Mary Phelps)

Books, Garden City, New Jersey, illus. by Sam Savitt, 1960, p. 106.

Chapter 8

Negotiating Your Purchase

The terms of private sale are as varied as the people who enter into an agreement with each other. Most horses bought at the track are sold strictly for cash with no home trial period, warranties or guarantees of soundness.

The price you can expect to pay for a Thoroughbred will range all the way from the meat price, around 50 or 60 cents a pound or $500 to $600 for an average horse, up to the claiming price which starts around $1,200 at smaller tracks. The price is influenced by location. At tracks in Thoroughbred oriented areas such as Maryland, or the portion of West Virginia bordering on Virginia, serviceably sound horses will bring a better price than in the Midwest where Western riding predominates and the Quarter Horse is king.

Age, sex, soundness, size and conformation all have a bearing on the price. Most prices are subject to negotiation. A big, good looking, athletic horse will bring the claiming price, or close to it, while the small, weedy rat can be had for next to nothing. An expensively dressed buyer who drives a fancy car is likely to be quoted a higher price than the shopper in faded Levis, old boots and an out-at-the-elbows sweater driving a battered, dusty Chevy pickup.

It is a good idea to take color Polaroid photos of any of the horses you are seriously considering, with a note on the back of the picture including the horse's name, age, asking price, trainer's name and stall location. It is surprising and distressing how this information can slip away by the time you get home and try to go over mentally all you have seen and done in a day. How sad to find a horse you really like, only to be unable to remember his name or where you saw him!

When you have found a horse without obvious defect and with a kind and friendly nature, by all means have him vetted. It is advisable to make arrangements with your own veterinarian to go to the track to pass judgement on your prospective purchase. Do not ask the small animal person who cares for your dog or cat; he will be more knowledgeable about hamsters and budgies than horses, while a vet with a mixed large animal practice will see more cattle, sheep and swine than he will horses in the course of a day's work. Select a veterinarian who specializes in horses. If you do not know of one, ask for advice at several well run stables or breeding farms in your area. Chances are the names of one or two veterinarians will be on everyone's list. Get in touch with him and find when and if he is willing to examine the horse for soundness. If he is unable to examine the horse, perhaps he can suggest the name of another equine practioner who can. If you can plan to go with him, it will be an educational experience for you. Make sure to plan a time convenient to the trainer. Arrange for an exercise rider to gallop the horse so his heart and lungs can be checked both before and after exercise. If the trainer refuses to allow this part of the exam, it should alert you to the fact that some problem may exist.

There are many equine specialists practicing at the racetrack. If you find it more convenient than bringing a veterinarian in from the outside, chose one who is not the seller's veterinarian in order to avoid a conflict of interest situation. It is more business-like to obtain the opinion of an independent expert. You can obtain a list of vets licensed to practice at a track by inquiring at the racing secretary's office.

You will not be permitted to take the horse around the track yourself unless you are licensed as an exercise rider by the state in which the racetrack is located. This restriction is for the safety of everyone involved. Riders are licensed only after they have demonstrated their ability to ride and are fully familiar with the rules of the racetrack. The purpose of having the horse galloped is to observe how he moves and how he tolerates exercise. The examining veterinarian will listen to his heart and lungs both before and after exercise. Many heart murmurs are functional, rather than organic (caused by a physical defect or abnormality); although they can be heard when the horse is at rest, they disappear when the heart speeds up as it does when the horse gallops. A horse's respiration may sound normal at rest, but abnormal noises may occur when the lungs expand fully at exercise.

The cost of the examination should be discussed in advance. The cost should be around $150 to $200 depending upon the number of miles the veterinarian must travel and what, if any, X-rays or ultrasound scans are necessary to form a valid opinion. Blood testing to determine what, if any medication the horse may be on will add considerably to the cost of the examination.

Negotiate to include the Jockey Club foal certificate in the sale. Possession of the foal certificate establishes the horse's age, identity and parentage; it enhances his resale value. It is particularly important that the "papers" go with any animal intended for breeding.

The markings and color on the foal certificate should match the markings on the animal under consideration. The lip tattoo on the horse should correspond with the animal's registration number. The first two digits of that number are replaced in the tattoo by a letter. The letters continue in sequence and are repeated every 26 years. For instance, if the registration number is 801142, the tattoo should be J1142; 84 is replaced with N on the tattoo, 87 with Q. Another series will begin with A in 1997.

The location of cowlicks, or whorls in the horse's coat, is another means of identifying Thoroughbreds. The location of each cowlick is listed on the horse's foal certificate. Identifying their exact place is of particular importance on a horse with no white markings. Lip tattoos become illegible with age, often leaving the whorls as the only key to positive identification. Cowlicks are commonly located on the horse's face, on his neck near the mane and in the jugular groove. There may also be cowlicks on the front of the neck and on the chest. The whorls by the stifles which all horses have are not listed, nor are the whorls under the fetlock.

In some racing jurisdictions, photographs of the horse's "night eyes" or chestnuts are used in identification. These horny projections on the inner aspect of the legs, above the knees and below the hocks, are as individual as human finger prints and do not alter with age.

The certificate of registration also lists the state of a horse's birth; the date on which he was tattooed; if a male, whether he has been castrated; the name of the horse's breeder (owner of the foal's dam at the time of foaling) and the name of the person to whom the certificate was originally issued. The reverse of the document lists transfers of ownership, whether by sale or claim, with the address of each owner; it is possible to get in touch with your new horse's former owners to learn more about his previous life and history. Changes of ownership by claim will all be documented as will private transfers at the track; racing jurisdictions require a bill of sale as proof of purchase before allowing a horse to race under a new owner's name. Private individuals are sometimes careless in respect to this detail; a sale from a farm or training center may not have been recorded.

Often the owner is reluctant to give up the foal certificate, although it is plainly stated thereon, "This certificate to be preserved and transferred to purchaser gratis if this horse is sold. Possession and presentation of this certificate is a requirement to race or breed the horse it identifies. Record transfer on reverse side." The reason for reluctance to part with the foal certificate is that the horse may have been bought, "on the cuff;" that is, he may have been sold on time, with the payments to come from future purses. Since the horse cannot race unless his papers are in the racing secretary's office at the track where he is to start, retaining the papers prevent his earning money for which the original purchaser would become liable.

The foal certificate is not necessary in order to show unless the class is restricted to Thoroughbreds. It is useful to have should you wish to sell the horse, since it positively establishes his age and identity. Although the certificate of registration is not needed to participate in most activities, it is a nice thing to have and you should obtain it, if possible.

Jockey club certificate and details concerning it

From Racetrack to Hunt Field

Faith and Credit (High Drag-Mi-Gal-Sue by Hearts Away) a 16:1 hand bay mare foaled in 1979 had a modestly successful race career, winning 6 of 34 starts and $22,188. After producing one foal, she was sold to Randy Waterman, steeplechase rider and whip for the Piedmont Fox Hounds, Upperville, Virginia where she has performed well as a staff horse under the rigors of long, hard hunting seasons. (Photo courtesy Chris Christenson)

Chapter 9

Buying at Auction

Auctions of Thoroughbreds of racing age are often offered at racetracks, usually at the end of a race meeting. Horses of racing age are also included in mixed sale catalogues (a mixed sale is one which includes horses of all ages and sexes). *The Blood-Horse, Thoroughbred Times, The Daily Racing Form, Horsemen's Journal* and various state magazines devoted to Thoroughbred racing all list upcoming sales as a regular feature (See Appendix IV). Anyone may attend an auction. To bid, you must first establish credit with the sales company. Usually a letter of credit from your bank is required.

Although the prospective buyer may look the horse over in the stable area and may have him jogged before the horse goes in the ring, there will be no chance of trying the horse under saddle. Do not display your inexperience by asking to do so since you will certainly be refused. There are no guarantees of soundness unless expressly announced at the time of sale. Horses which have defective vision, are bleeders or cribbers must be so announced at the time of sale or the horse is subject to return by the buyer. Any animal sold as a colt which is actually a gelding or a ridgling, or one which is described as a gelding, which is actually a ridgling or colt, is also subject to return. A ridgling is a male horse with one or both testicles undescended. Although the accessible testicle has usually been removed, rendering him sterile (spermatogenesis does not take place at body temperature, only in the cooler temperature of the scrotum) he retains the stallion temperament due to continued production of testosterone from the remaining testicle.   Similarly, a horse on the steward's, starters, veterinarian's list, or which has been nerved must be so announced at time of sale or be subject to return. Horses on the starter's list are horses which refuse to break from the gate or which behave in a dangerous or unruly manner. They are barred from further racing until they have had additional schooling and "get their ticket" to start again. Horses on the steward's list have run in an erratic manner so as to endanger other horses and riders in a race. Horses on the vet's list are not racing sound. A nerved horse is one in which the posterior digital nerve has been severed to relieve intractable pain in the foot.

The registration papers must be furnished by the seller in order to enter the horse in the sale.

Beyond the above safeguards, the bidder "buys 'em as he sees 'em." With a good eye and good luck, the buyer can find a suitable prospect at a reasonable price. An auction offers the buyer an assortment of horses to look over, compare and from which to choose. At the front of the sales catalog are listed the terms of the sale. Be sure to read these pages carefully, making certain that you understand exactly what the rules state. You are presumed to have read and understood the rules and are bound to abide by them if you wish to bid. The sales catalogue will have a three generation pedigree of the horse being sold, remarks about his sire, both as a racehorse and as a sire, and sometimes as many as 4 generations of runners under the female line, plus the subject horse's own racing record. As a general rule, the horse must be paid for before leaving the grounds.

At most auctions there is an upset price or minimum opening bid. If such a bid is not immediately forthcoming, the horse is passed out of the ring unsold. The upset price can vary from $100 at non-select mixed sales to $10,000 at the select summer sales of yearlings. In a select sale, each entry has been approved by a committee of experts as to pedigree and inspected at the farm by another expert to determine that the youngster has proper conformation.

At the more prominent sales, there will be several

independent veterinarians on the grounds who have no affiliation with either the sales company or the consignor. It is wise, with the seller's permission, to have the horse vetted before he goes into the ring to sell. All sales become final at the fall of the hammer with the above noted exceptions.

There will be spotters, or bid takers working the crowd as the auctioneer asks the audience to bid again. "Hey, boys, Look-a-here, Grand looking big horse, here. He'p yo'self. Don't let him get away from you. Six, Six, Six! I got 5. Who'll gimmee Six, Six, Six?" Pay attention to the amount the auctioneer is actually asking for; he will try to make it seem that the bidding has passed to a higher figure. Do not be fooled into bidding against yourself; it can happen under the hypnotic spell of the auctioneer's chant. If you feel unsure of yourself, ask someone you trust who is experienced to do the bidding for you. Bids may go up by increments of $100, $1,000 or $10,000, not by $1 or $10. Make sure you know what you are agreeing to before nodding to the spotter who will try to make you feel as if you are a cheapskate if you hesitate to bid again on a horse he has seen that you like. Pay careful attention or you are likely to end up contracting to pay more than you had intended. The spotter will hand you a contract to sign immediately while your enthusiasm from bidding is still undiminished. After the hammer has fallen, the horse is yours and it is too late to change your mind.

There will be representatives of several horse transportation companies to van your new purchase home for you. These people are professionals and it is money well spent to leave the driving to one of them.

Pow! Wow! Zap! It's Mighty Mouse!

Annette Murphy's Mighty Mouse, registered name Nalpac (Listen to Reason-Parisian Blue by Mr. Jive) foaled in 1975, was raced off the farm until he was ten, winning 3 of 81 starts, placing third 5 times, for earnings of $12,182. He has been used in the hunting field as a whip's horse for 4 seasons and does dressage and eventing. Annette has recently been giving riding lessons to young beginners on him. Small for a Thoroughbred, Mighty Mouse stands a scant 15 hands. (Photo courtesy Lydia McCullough)

Chapter 10

How Racetrack Training Affects Reschooling

In buying a former racehorse, you reap the benefits of years of meticulous care. However, other factors in the horse's previous experience will prove to offer impediments to his reschooling.

Thoroughbreds on well-run farms are handled from birth. At one or two days of age, they are fitted with a foal halter which is checked daily for fit and adjusted as necessary. They are taught to lead at an early age, first following the mare to and from pasture, then later, on their own. They grow rapidly on lush, tree shaded, safely fenced pastures; they are encouraged to eat all the grain they will readily consume, often fed in a "creep", a pen into which a foal can enter, but not a mare. Their feet are trimmed monthly, or more often if corrective work is being done. They are wormed at four to six week intervals. They receive preventive shots to guard against the many infectious diseases young horses are subject to and their teeth are checked regularly by a veterinarian specializing in equine dentistry who will file down any irritating sharp edges and remove troublesome wolf teeth. Some farms weigh their young horses on a regular basis to make sure that each youngster is making a satisfactory weight gain. Careful records are maintained, not only of them, but of all their near and not so near relatives. In short, no expense or care is spared so that they may achieve their full potential as athletes.

Late in the yearling year, usually after the fall yearling sales, the young Thoroughbreds are broken to saddle under the supervision of an expert. The riders are very lightweight and must be agile as well as tactful. No rough methods are condoned; the yearlings are firmly but kindly handled. A long time is spent walking and jogging, usually with a trainer riding along side on a quiet pony who will serve as role model for the pupils. When the youngsters are thoroughly bridle wise, they are taken on to a training track for more jogging and some slow gallops. Other trainers prefer to take their charges quietly across the fields and through the woods because hacking out is less boring than going round and round a track. The slow work continues through the fall and early winter, though some of the more mature colts may have short breezes and trials against each other to get ready for their two-year-old season.

During this breaking and early training the young Thoroughbred becomes accustomed to many strange sights and sounds which would upset the average pleasure horse. He has been trained to walk up a loading ramp early in his career and has probably been shipped countless times from farm to auction sale to training center and from track to track. The racehorse will be easy to load on a van and will be far more cooperative than the average horse because he knows what to expect. There is a very good chance, however, that although he knows all about shipping by van, he may never have set foot in a trailer. Assume that this is the case and do not become impatient if he hesitates going into a trailer.

Most former runners are used to traffic - cars, trucks, vans, dumpsters and motorcycles, having seen them all at the racetrack. They are accustomed to crowds, other horses and such distractions.

A racehorse will show the results of years of painstaking grooming. His coat will shine like burnished metal. He is used to a daily bath which usually consists of being hosed off thoroughly or being sponged over with water containing a body brace. Soap is not used for the daily bath since it tends to remove the natural oils from the horse's coat. Racehorses enjoy their daily bath so cooperation while being bathed is another benefit derived from years of handling.

Racehorses are used to having their feet handled and are, as a rule, very well mannered about being shod. Tooth floating and minor veterinary procedures hold no fear for them. Drawing blood, routine vaccination and tube worming are accomplished without a hassle.

In buying a former racehorse, you are acquiring a thoroughly handled rather sophisticated animal that has been everywhere and seen everything--almost. In certain ways, his previous experience is disadvantageous to his new role as sport or pleasure horse.

Due to being confined to a stall and the generally unnatural life which the horse led at the racetrack, the runner has often developed unpleasant mannerisms, some of which are more serious and long lasting than others.

All up and down the shed rows at the track, as horses are being walked, the horses in the stalls reach out menacingly, ears flattened, teeth bared, making biting gestures at the passers-by. Some horses squeal and grind their teeth. Others lash out with their heels or rear and strike. Such aggressive territorial display may be directed at horses only, or may also include people. Horses which actually savage passers-by are required to have a stall screen of heavy wire mesh.

Runners lead a life of extreme tension alternating with ineffable boredom. Each day they are out of their stalls for only an hour or an hour and a half at most. To help pacify them, many trainers keep a radio constantly playing. The horses learn many little games of their own to help pass the time; when their pastimes become harmful to their health or dangerous to their handlers, they are known as stable vices (as opposed to vices under saddle).

Cribbing is one of the most common vices. The cribber fixes his front teeth on any projection he can reach; the stall door or the edge of his feed tub are common objects for the horse to grab. As he bites, he sucks and swallows air with a characteristic grunting sound. The habit of cribbing is said to interfere with the horse's digestion and to make it difficult for him to maintain his weight. Mighty Kelso was a cribber as was

Halo and his Kentucky Derby winning son Sunny's Halo. If I really liked a horse, the fact that he was a cribber would not deter me from buying him. The habit can be controlled by the wearing a cribbing strap or a cage-like muzzle, neither of which interfere with eating or drinking. The most undesirable aspect of cribbing is that it is a habit readily picked up from one horse by another, much as smoking is among a group of young people. Mares that crib pass the habit on to their foals by example, not by heredity as has been suggested by some writers. Occasionally, if the habit has not been long standing, freedom may effect a cure. The three-year old filly Esterette was a cribber when she came to us from the racetrack, but dropped the habit as soon as she was turned out in a nice green field. Other horses give up the vice, only to resume the habit when confined for long periods or subjected to other forms of stress, just as the former smoker will reach for his cigarettes, seeking oral gratification in a time of unusual tension. Burglary, however, who loved the life at the racetrack which was his home for eight years, except for brief holidays on the farm, took up cribbing upon his retirement, finding life on the farm to be a bore. He cribbed on his fence boards while looking down the road for a van to take him back to where the action was.

Chewing and wood biting are distinct from cribbing but may be the forerunner of it. The habit is common in young horses who are shedding their baby teeth. It often persists as something to do when there is nothing to do, like a child picking a scab off his knee or peeling the wallpaper beside his bed. The horse chews anything he can reach - feed tubs, lead shanks or other items of tack carelessly left within his reach. Some horses rub their teeth along any available edge, eventually wearing them down to the gum.

Weaving, bobbing and stall walking are related vices. They consist of a stylized pattern of aimless motion, like the repetitive, nervous activity of the great cats at the zoo. The weaver sways back and forth from side to side. The bobber nods his head, often with a stamp of a foot. The walker either paces up and down or in endless circles wearing a trough in the floor of his stall. Each horse dances his own individual pattern to the distress of his groom who despairs of keeping the stall looking as it should. Many devices are used to help prevent this useless expenditure of energy. Sometimes a plastic pop bottle or milk container is hung on a string to disturb the weaver's ritual pattern. Bales of straw are put in the walker's path to interfere with his endless journey. Usually the weavers, bobbers and walkers are not deterred from their activities, merely incorporating the obstacles as part of the pattern. Tying the horse for part of the day is the only method of bringing his gyrations to a temporary halt. Like cribbing, the above vices are readily imitated by other horses and thus are doubly undesirable. Fortunately, most horses give up weaving, bobbing and walking when they spend all or part of their day at liberty, although they may resume them when feeling unhappy or insecure. For instance, when moved to unfamiliar surroundings or when separated from a favorite companion they may resort to a former stall vice. Others maintain their addiction and you can see them weaving in front of their paddock gate, walking up and down the fence or in circles that would fit inside a twelve by twelve foot stall, or head bobbing by their fence feeder. The latter may be only to remind their inattentive handlers that it is, indeed, time to be fed.

Kicking the stall partition is a sign of irritability most often seen at feeding time and translates as, "Hurry it up, stupid!" Like other undesirable habits, it tends to diminish when the horse spends more time at liberty. Kicking the stall wall seems to be unrelated to the vice of kicking at other horses.

Although your former racehorse has been groomed and handled from his earliest days, because he is on the muscle and feeling sharp, he may attempt to kick or nip playfully while being curried. Speak soothingly to him. Make certain you are not tickling him - many horses are very ticklish. This behavior is due to an excess of high spirits rather than meanness.

Many horses will break out in a sweat or begin to quiver with anticipation when they see the tack. This behavior will soon be replaced with calmness if he is reassured rather than reprimanded. The horse associates the rider carrying his tack with the excitement of going to the racetrack to gallop, work or race. He is literally quivering with excitement and anticipation. This behavior is a conditioned response not unlike the reflexive salivation of Ivan Petrovitch Pavlov's famous dogs who learned to drool at the sound of a bell. The Pavlovian horse should be patted and spoken to softly. For several days he should be lead around for a few minutes at a time with the tack on before being put away. Eventually he will become nonchalant about seeing you with your saddle and bridle draped over your arm. Make certain that your body language is not causing him concern. Be low key with him and he will soon relax with you.

Unfortunately, not all trainers, grooms and exercise riders are patient, kind and skillful. As in other occupations, there are good, bad and indifferent individuals. If your horse has changed hands frequently, it is likely that somewhere along the line he may have been subjected to rough handling. His subsequent behavior will reflect this fact. Many horses try to nip when the girth is tightened, no doubt in retaliation for having been pinched in the past. The horse who has had his eye poked by a buckle while being bridled and his ears none too gently stuffed into the head stall will not be a model of cooperation while being bridled. Most vices are far easier to prevent than to cure. Taking the bridle apart and assembling it again on the horse's head with great gentleness, much praise and even the feeding of a special treat, will surely effect a cure.

A horse coming from the track will have a strong desire to run, especially when in company. He thinks this is what is expected of him and it will take careful, patient training to overcome that belief. How long the horse was in training, how successful a racehorse he was, his temperament, his age, as well as your skill and tact will determine how long it will be before he gets rid of the notion that every equine gathering is a horse race. Remember, even at the racetrack, long slow gallops were by far more frequent than works, breezes or actual competition. Your former racehorse has learned to take his cue as to what to do from his rider. Make certain you do not give him signals you do not intend. For instance, if you are tensed up and apprehensive about being run off with, he will feel the tightness in your hands and legs and think you are telling him it is time to take hold of the bit and fly. Many former runners take to hacking as if they had never done anything else, while others require a year or more to make the adjustment from track to hack. Some never do.

The ex-racehorse has gained the reputation of being too hot for other purposes. The same complaint can be leveled at any horse at a high level of fitness, whether for polo, endurance riding or racing. According to Olympic gold medalist, Jim Day, "You just don't ever come across a dead fit horse in normal show horse activity. If the new owner tries to train him when he's fit and really sharp, the horse is going to act fresh and be really difficult. The owner could probably ride him for two hours and the horse still wouldn't get tired so the rider's not going to teach him very much until he can get his brain to where it is in a thinking state. To do that takes a little understanding."[1]

Although the racehorse is thoroughly sophisticated about such potentially frightening things as vans, trucks, cars and people in large numbers, he will be completely naive in regard to the every day objects at the average farm, riding stable or suburban home. When Nichols W. first came to us, he did not look twice at a huge semi lumbering down the road at 60 miles an hour but broke out in a sweat at the sight of a child on a tricycle. Similarly, Sir Olton, who looked half asleep in the middle of all noisy hustle and bustle at the track, was panicked at the sight of the goats standing on top of their house to nibble tender leaves and blossoms from an over hanging apple branch, or doing a tap dance on top of the hood of a car. A child on roller skates, a kite fluttering in the wind, an overturned lawn chair - or even an upright one - a field full of cattle switching their tails in unison, a tea towel flapping on a kitchen clothesline, a garden tractor or a lawn mower are unfamiliar to most racehorses and are, therefore, potentially dangerous and thus frightening. Bridges, culvert pipes, running streams, barking dogs, squawking chickens and steep ditches, all of which the pleasure horse takes for granted will be strange to the former runner. Allowances must be made for him to become accustomed to his new surroundings.

---

[1] Jefferies, *loc. cit.*, p. 11

Chief Leads the Pack

Another Thoroughbred owned by Annette Murphy and her husband,, is Chief (Glow Native by Shy Native-Glow of Dawn by Misty Flight), foaled in 1974. The 16:3 hand chestnut gelding started an astounding 169 times in a career that spanned 10 seasons. He won 26 races, was second and third 27 times each for earnings of $220,867. Truly an iron horse, he started as many as 29 times in a single season. Chief bowed a tendon in his last race at the age of 11. After a year's rest he began a new life as a staff horse in the hunt field, first as the huntsman's horse for three seasons and then as a whip's horse. "He is an incredibly tough horse and can hunt for hours without tiring," according to his proud owner.[1] (Photo courtesy Annette Murphy)

---

[1] Annette Murphy, Landrum, South Carolina, letter, May, 1990.

Chapter 11

When You Get Him Home

When your new horse arrives from the track, put him in a box stall with hay and water. Leave him alone to settle down from the van ride, get used to his new surroundings and begin to feel comfortable and secure in them. A couple of hours later, bring him an apple cut in quarters or slices of raw carrot to show him your intentions are friendly. Sit with him until he gets used to your company. Take your portable radio and a magazine along and sit quietly outside his stall till he makes friendly overtures to you. Play the radio very softly. He will be curious about it. Speak quietly to him, but let him make the first gesture of friendship to which you can respond by a gentle word or another slice of carrot. A bond of friendship will form between you which will be very helpful in your future work with him. The famous horse tamer of outlaw horses, Rarey, said, "It is best to have the horse of one's party," meaning that horse and rider should be on the same team, or partners.

Do not crosstie your former racehorse. At the racetrack, the shedrows and barn aisles are kept open so horses may walk in them. Horses are tied in their stalls to a ring bolt. If you crosstie your horse, he is likely to pull back, rear up and flip. If you tie him in his stall, make certain that you tie him to something secure, such as a ring bolt, which you can buy at any tack or farm supply store, or to one of the sturdy studs or uprights which support the barn. Do not tie him to the stall door, grill work, stall screen, feeder or manger. If you think you must crosstie him, begin by cross tying him in his stall, so if he wants to pull back, he will back into a wall. In cross tying him in the aisle of the barn, begin at a blind end, or with the door shut so if he pulls back he will stop himself. Do not tie him at the open end of the barn where he is likely to be startled by horses and people, as well as vehicles, coming and going.

After you and your new horse have become acquainted, he should be taken out and walked quietly in hand so that he can have a chance to see and get used to all the unfamiliar things. For added security, it is wise to pass the chain of the shank over his nose, a procedure he is already used to and which gives you more control should he become upset by something he sees. Don't have a death grip on him so the chain hurts his nose. Be relaxed and chances are he will be too. He should be allowed to take his time in going past anything that seems to frighten him. Talk quietly to him and pat him if he is nervous. After a little while he will relax, drop his head and eat grass.

Your horse will be easier to retrain when he has had an ample chance to unwind, which he cannot accomplish by staying in his box stall. The best way to unwind is to be turned out. Because he has been kept up for a long time, in many instances since he was a yearling, there is a risk of his hurting himself. The risk, however, is more than offset by the benefits he will derive. In turning him out for the first time, it will be helpful to have him lightly tranquilized. Your equine veterinarian will advise you on this matter. It will be helpful to longe him at a slow trot for 15 minutes or so to take the edge off his exuberance. Most Thoroughbreds have been taught to longe at some time during their careers, probably as part of their early breaking. It is advisable to longe him in an enclosure of some sort. An indoor riding hall or a round pen, such as is used in breaking a young horse, is ideal but a small, level paddock is fine. Don't choose the paddock next to the yearlings or other silly young horses, since they will do their best to incite him to riot. And don't forget to lock up the dogs!

Before turning your new horse out, have his racing shoes pulled. Racing shoes are made of aluminum with steel toe grabs to help the horse in digging in with his toes to get a fast start out of the gate. Many racing shoes also have heel caulks or stickers. These projections can cut and bruise his fetlocks and tendons as he cuts up when first at liberty. They are also very dangerous to any other horse with which he may be turned out. Horses racing in very close company have had their tendons severed by another horse's toe grab - or his own if he must be checked sharply.

If he seems to be uncomfortable barefoot - and most are not - he can be shod with plain steel plates in front only.

When turning him loose for the first time, choose a calm day. Horses are excited by motion. On a windy day everything is in motion. When the wind is whipping the branches of the trees into a frenzy and waste paper is blowing about, even sedate, elderly broodmares gallop around with their tails in the air. The footing should be firm and dry. Because the horse is certain to cut plain and fancy capers when first turned loose, he is likely to fall and injure himself if the ground is slippery. In winter, a heavy snow will provide a good cushion and will also slow his progress. Ice, mud and frozen ground are treacherous and should be avoided.

When you turn your horse out for the first time, do not put him in a large field, but, rather into a small, stoutly fenced corral, small paddock, or that indoor arena or round pen you longed him in. The fence should be made of heavy oak boards or pressure treated pine, stout poles or heavy gauge woven (not welded) wire with a top board. Barbed wire or flimsy stock fence with large spaces and a top strand of barbed wire are dangerous. Because their binocular vision is restricted (their depth perception is virtually nil), horses often fail to see a wire fence until it is too late to stop or turn. The presence of a board, rather than barbed wire on top of a wire fence makes the barrier easier to see. In a large field, the horse can get going so fast that he is out of control and cannot stop in time to avoid running into the fence. For these reasons, a small, safely fenced paddock or corral is a far better place for a first turn out than a spacious pasture.

Any moveable objects should be taken outside the fence. The horse might injure himself on metal feed tubs, water tubs or farm machinery.

On first being turned out, your horse will gallop, buck, kick, squeal, snort and pound around with his tail in the air. He will make incredible turns and breath taking sliding stops. He may hit the fence a couple of times and for this reason, it must be stout enough not to break or splinter, otherwise he might be badly cut. When he has worked up a good sweat, he will roll, shake himself and start the same process all over again, but with diminishing vigor. A few horses will run up and down the fence the entire day that they are first turned out, or even for several days. Throw your horse some hay to pacify him. Offer him water from a bucket, a few sips at a time.

After a few days, when he is accustomed to the small paddock and behaving calmly in it, he may be put out in a larger enclosure. If it is late fall or winter, when the grass is dry and sparse, he may spend half a day at pasture without ill effect. In the spring and summer, however, when the grass is luxuriant, he should not have access to it for more than an hour or he will eat more than is good for him. At the track, he ate hay rather than grass. Gradually increase the time he is at grass each day. Even with care, his manure will be loose until his digestive system adjusts to the change in diet.

Before taking your new horse home, it is a good idea to find out how much of what kind of feed he has been getting so his customary feed can be duplicated for a few days and then gradually withdrawn as you substitute the type of feed you are used to giving. If you cannot find out what he has been getting, it is safe to give him all the grass hay (as opposed to legume hay such as clover or alfalfa) which he will clean up in a reasonable time. If he paws, bangs the stall door, whinnies and frets, he is telling you he needs more to eat. If he merely sorts through the hay, looking for choice morsels, while wasting half of it, he is getting too much, or maybe you are not feeding the quality of hay he is used to. Start off feeding him only a small quantity of grain twice, or preferably three times a day. He can make better use of grain fed in small quantities than in large. It is difficult to suggest an ideal amount. Horses differ so much in their utilization of feed that what is perfect for one will be too much for another, or not enough for a third. Because of his significantly higher metabolism, a Thoroughbred will burn up more energy than a cold blooded horse, and, thus, require more calories to maintain his condition or still more to gain weight. It is probably wiser to let him get more of his calories from high quality hay than from grain. Alfalfa hay can be included in his hay ration for more calories, as can hay made from orchard grass. Corn and corn oil are good sources of energy and lend a good sheen to the coat. It is inadvisable to feed cracked corn to horses. Whole kernel corn or, if you can find it, ear corn are preferable since they are less likely to cause impaction than cracked corn. At the track, your horse probably had been getting a bran mash several times a week to offset the constipating effect of eating dry forage. Offer him a one pound coffee can of bran once a day with his grain ration. When he is maintained on pasture, the bran can be eliminated from his diet since it will no longer be needed. Remember that "The eye of the master maketh the horse fat." Play it by ear. Do not feed him what your friend is feeding his horse, for their needs may be entirely different. His feed should be relevant only to his condition and the energy level at which he is performing. Adjust his feed toward the ideal condition you have in mind for him.

Too many new horse owners fall into the trap of the "Nice Horsey Syndrome." They equate food with love. Be careful that you do not overfeed your horse. If his energy input exceeds his exercise, you are likely to have an overly fresh horse, one who will want to play or act up rather than paying attention to his lessons. He will be, quite literally, "feeling his oats." The underexercised - overfed horse becomes a menace to all concerned. Because he is difficult, if not downright nasty, to ride, he will be ridden less, compounding the problem. His health as well as his manners are in jeopardy; laminitis, heart, kidney and respiratory ailments are all unwelcome sequels to injudicious feeding.

Salt should be available to him at all times. It may be provided in an individual 4 pound salt block in his feed tub, a pasture block in his pasture, or loose in a sheltered mineral box, if you live in a dry climate. A pinch of loose salt can be added to his grain. An occasional horse will bite large chunks from his salt block. We had one gelding who moistened his salt block with a mouthful of water making it easier to destroy, creating an unholy mess. An excess of salt is undesirable. The horse who eats his salt block should not have salt free choice, but should have a pinch of salt sprinkled over his grain, once a day or more often in extremely hot weather. Salt containing trace minerals will supply the minerals which may be deficient in the soil (and hence the grass and hay) of your area. Make certain the salt is formulated for horses rather than cattle since certain minerals added for cattle are toxic to horses.

Caution should be taken in turning out your retired racehorse with other horses. Before putting him with a group, allow him to buddy up with one other horse. Select a quiet, patient, non-aggressive older gelding. Allow them to become good friends before introducing them to a larger group. Possibly your horse has not had a companion since the time he was a yearling. He may be totally ignorant of normal equine manners. He may be very timid and shy. On the other hand, he may be unduly aggressive. The timid horse who is willing to take his place at the end of the line is far less likely to be injured by other horses than is the individual with a well developed ego who wishes to be high man on the totem pole. The social climber must challenge or be challenged by each horse in the herd, eyeball - to - eyeball. The horse which retreats when ears are flattened, teeth bared and hooves cocked, loses status. Most herds of horses display a straight line dominance with one boss, usually a wise old mare to whom all the others are subservient. The number two horse, usually the old mare's best friend and companion, yields only to her, and so on down the line to the bottom of the pecking order (so called, because the straight line dominance was first observed and described in a flock of chickens who assert status by pecking those lower down the social order). It is inevitable that a little hide be lost in the reestablishment of the herd's hierarchy which is disturbed when a new member joins the group. As a rule, things sort themselves out very quickly. Horses, however, who seem to have an undying hatred for each other should be separated

96

before any permanent injury can happen.

If you should bring home an uncastrated colt, he must be kept in a paddock by himself. It must have a high, stout fence, preferably double fenced, so he cannot touch noses with other horses or make other contact with them or he he will pick fights with the geldings and try to cover the mares, if any. I have seen a half-dozen 5-year old Lippizzaner stallions turned out together, but they had all been friends and companions since earliest foalhood. Their posturing with each other and territorial display were all in fun.

The same restrictions apply to a recently castrated gelding. Since motile spermatazoa are still stored in his seminal vesicles for several days, he can impregnate a receptive mare. He will be rank and aggressive with other male horses until the testosterone circulating in his bloodstream is dissipated - several months, at least.

Because they have been shut off from free association with other horses for most of their lives, former racehorses form intense friendships when given the opportunity. Their devotion may become so intense as to be a nuisance. They fret when separated, and even when in the company of other horses, run up and down the fence, calling frantically. An occasional horse will become so very upset that he is in danger of injuring himself. He must be shut up in the barn if the other horse goes off without him. Creche and Beverly Blue, who were six and seven at the time, became very devoted to each other. When Creche was sold, Beverly Blue continued to call and to look hopefully down the road in the direction he had gone for almost a year, until she had produced a lively foal which then took up all her attention.

Intoxicated with his new-found freedom, your new horse may be reluctant to be caught when you want him. He will be easier to catch if you form the habit of giving him a treat when you come for him. Start the practice while he is still in the small paddock. If he resists being caught in the larger enclosure, feeding some of what you have brought along for him to his companions will prove to be more than flesh can bear. Be sure you give him what you have offered. You will be able to fool him once, but not again. Once you have him in the barn, give him a handful of grain in his feed box so he will associate being caught and taken into the barn as a pleasant experience rather than merely the temporary loss of his precious, new-found freedom.

Flies at the racetrack are not a problem to the same degree as at the average farm or boarding stable. At the racetrack, the stalls are picked out several times a day. Manure and wet, soiled bedding are removed from the stable area daily. The shedrows are fogged periodically with an insecticide. The solution with which the horses are sponged off after exercise usually contains an insect repellent.

Unless the stalls, paddocks and areas around your barn are picked up daily, the fly population will explode by mid-summer; it will not subside until after the first frost. Since manure is an ideal breeding ground for flies of all kinds, it should not be piled up, as it too often is, near stalls and paddocks. Preferably, it should be spread on pastures where other species of livestock graze, or on fields where crops will be harvested. If your horse is kept in a rural area, a neighboring farmer would welcome your barn cleanings for his fields. If your area is more suburban than rural, try to find a mushroom grower. Horse manure is the essential medium for propagating edible mushrooms commercially. Mushroom growers will even pick up your accumulated horse droppings. If you use straw or peat moss for bedding; they may even pay you for it. The mushroom growing industry in the United States is centered in the Kennett Square, New Bolton, Chad's Ford area of Pennsylvania, just a little northwest of Philadelphia; they will travel long distances to obtain horse manure if it is available in sufficient quantities, so check it out.

If you must store manure on the premises, have a pit constructed of masonry - cinder or cement block (not wood, since it will rot) - with a wheel barrow ramp to the top. Cover the manure bin with a tarp. Both your horses and your neighbors will thank you.

With his thin skin and short, fine hair, the retired runner will suffer cruelly from flies during his first summer on the farm, unless he has a cool place to stand during the heat of the day. For this reason, many people prefer to bring their horses in during the day and turn them out in the cool of the evening. After the first year, the horse will develop a certain degree of tolerance to the toxins which insects inject when they suck blood. Until he does, he will be covered with welts and weals which he may rub hairless by scratching them. The gelding, Deb's Gold, wallowed in the muck at the shallow end of the pond until he had covered his whole body with a soothing, protective layer of mud. There are a number of insect repellents on the market which you can apply to your horse's coat; make certain the product you buy is safe for horses and, if necessary, that you dilute it according to the directions on the label. Insecticides and repellents formulated for other species are not necessarily safe for horses. Chestnut horses have more sensitive skin than bays, browns and grays, so use care. Poor Standoff, a chestnut, was being tormented by flies. He was carelessly sponged off with a repellant compounded for cattle. He lost all his body hair, became severely sunburned, lost large areas of skin and had to be kept in for much of the remainder of the summer, until the damage was repaired.

When the racehorse is turned out for the first time, he goes through an adjustment known as the let-down syndrome. At the track his metabolism was keyed to competition. His existence was predicated upon tension. The sudden removal of tension is both psychologically and physiologically challenging. The horse's blood-making system was dependent upon large and continuous out-pourings of adrenaline, set off by competition. When the stress of competition disappears, the production of adrenaline drops. The horse's blood making system which was in overdrive, shifts down to neutral. The horse may even become anemic. His glossy coat becomes harsh and dull. Instead of filling out the all too obvious humps and hollows of his frame, he becomes even thinner, although his intake of energy seems to be adequate. He may lose his appetite for a while.

The effects of the let-down syndrome can be lessened somewhat by daily, vigorous grooming and light exercise, either on a longe or under saddle. The let-down period is a normal transitional phase. It should not be a cause for alarm. Your vet may wish to suggest a tonic to improve the horse's appetite but, in time, the horse's metabolism will adjust to his new environment. He will begin to gain weight, but it may take several months to strike a new balance.

A Thoroughbred should never be kept in a tie stall - nor should any other horse, for that matter, if you care anything at all for him. He should have a loose box 12' by 12' or larger. Nor should he be kept in it except in extremes of weather. Horses which are confined for long periods of time stock up in the hind legs, or in all four legs. Remember, at the racetrack although the horse spent most of his time in a stall, he was exercised daily, even if the exercise was no more than being led around the shedrow at a walk for twenty minutes while his stall was being shaken out. While he stood idle, his legs were kept wrapped to prevent filling.

Although many barns have cement floors, they are unsuitable for horses. A cold, hard, unyielding surface is harmful to a horse's feet and legs, especially if he is shod. Urine tends to collect on cement floors; the stall becomes damp and clammy; where the ventilation is not ideal, ammonia fumes collect which are both unpleasant to smell and harmful to the lungs of the horse which breaths them. Cement floors are also slippery when wet, which they frequently are. There is a very real possibility that the combined effect of a hard, slippery surface and dampness will, in time, make any horse sore. It is likely to reaggravate a pre-existing arthritic condition which the former racehorse may have acquired from the stress of training.

The traditional flooring for stables is blue clay, well tamped. It offers a more resilient surface than either concrete or asphalt, so that it is easier on the horse's feet and legs. Clay drains somewhat better than either but not much better. It, too, tends to be slippery when wet and horses can readily dig holes in it.

We prefer a base of coarse gravel, covered with pea gravel, then crushed gravel, with powdered gravel or stone as the top layer. It can be tamped to make a firm, level surface. Sand should not be used, since the particles are round rather than irregular, they do not pack down. The surface remains uneven, and shifting and becomes mixed up in the bedding. Not only does much of it get thrown out, the mixture is frustrating to clean. Limestone is ideal where it is available, since it packs very well. Slate does well, too. Make use of whatever material is available locally. The cost will be determined by how far the material must be trucked to the site where it is needed. Check with a local building contractor to learn what he uses on driveways and where he gets it.

A stall floored with crushed rock offers excellent drainage, resilient footing and easy maintenance. To be sure, horses can and do paw holes in it. For such offenders, provide a stall mat. Most pawing is habitually done in one preferred area - by the door, feed tub or perhaps by the window, if it is low enough for him to see out. While a full-size heavy rubber stall mat 12' x 12' is ideal, it is very expensive, both to purchase and to have shipped to your barn. Since these mats are shipped in sections, however, and since most horses paw in only one preferred area, one mat can be used to pad several stalls. They are shipped in two 6' x 12' sections or three 4' x 12' sections. They are also made in ten foot modules. An alternative is to obtain, either new or used, strips of 3' wide industrial belting. A few inquiries to several local manufacturers may locate sources for industrial belting. Most of the major tire manufacturing companies also make industrial belting in a variety of widths and thicknesses.

The horse who roughs it out of doors is far more likely to stay fit, sound, healthy and happy than is the pampered horse who stays in his stall under a fancy blanket. But, you say, I want to show, hunt, event him and he looks too dreadful and is too hard to cool out with all that long hair. Then, keep his coat short, if you must, by turning him out in a New Zealand rug, a heavy, waterproof canvas blanket, lined with wool and with leg straps to keep it from slipping out of place.

During his racing career, your horse probably never had anything in his mouth more severe than a jointed snaffle with D rings, half checks, or large, round rings. Young horses race in a special cushion bit in which the mouth piece is padded and covered with leather. Other bits are merely a coarse chain covered by thick, soft rubber.

It would be the height of folly as well as cruelty to put a severe bit in the ex-racehorse's mouth. A twisted wire snaffle is a vicious bit, tricky to use even in the hands of a skilled professional and is certain to inflict damage in the hands of an amateur. The thinner the mouth piece, the more severe the bit, just as a sharp knife is more likely to cut than a dull one. A curb bit increases in severity in proportion to the length of the cheeks and the height of the port. The horse who is used to nothing more than a snaffle is likely to throw his head, back-up or even rear as an evasion and a protest when he feels the pain and unaccustomed pressure of a more severe bit. If the horse is too strong for the rider, or has a tendency to pull during the early stages of reschooling, a hackamore can be substituted for the bit as a temporary measure. A hackamore acts by pressure on the horse's nose and on the bones under the chin. It prevents mouth damage in a headstrong horse. The severe type of hackamore with curb chains levered by long shanks should be avoided.

It may be that a large hunting snaffle is all the bit your retired racehorse will ever need. If so, consider it a triumph. The more skilled the rider, the less he needs to depend on harsh controls. To put a long shanked Pelham or a double bridle with a severe curb bit on the horse for fear of being run away with and then to add a martingale to keep from being whacked in the nose by his head, is the kind of lethal foolishness in which many amateurs get themselves involved.

Some horses come from the track with relatively insensitive mouths. They are unresponsive to tactful direct rein pressure. For them a Kimberwicke (a type of Pelham, with a D ring, rather than a shank) gives slightly crisper control without the risk of adding to the damage already done. Failing that, a rubber covered Tom Thumb Pelham may be used. The Kimberwicke has been criticized as being neither fish nor fowl. Originally used as a jumper bit, it is discriminated against in hunter classes by certain judges. Be that as it may, some horses go better in a Kimberwicke than in any other bit. If it works, use it; if it doesn't try another.

For the horse who evades the bit by opening his mouth, a dropped nose band is the answer. Make certain that he is not evading the bit because of any roughness or irregularity of the bit, especially where it joins to the ring. A dropped noseband is used with a snaffle and must be carefully fitted below the bit, but not so low as to interfere with the horse's nostrils. The lower strap should lie in the chin groove. It must be tight enough to prevent crossing the jaws, but not so tight that the horse cannot flex his jaw. It should be possible to pass one finger under it, all the way around. A figure 8 nose band or an event model hinged noseband will have the same effect. A dropped noseband is also helpful on the horse who evades the bit by getting his tongue over it.

If the horse has the tendency to throw his head or to elevate his head to avoid the bit (stargaze), make certain that the bit you are using fits, has no rough edges, is not too severe and that your hands are light and responsive. After you have checked his equipment and found that it is not the source of his discomfort, you should have his teeth checked by an equine veterinarian, preferably one who specializes in dentistry to see if the cause of the problem could be his mouth. He may have sharp edges on his molars, wolf teeth, caps or another condition which could cause pain when pressure is applied to the bit.

Wolf teeth are vestigial premolars, occurring in front of the second premolars, most frequently in the upper jaw. Since wolf teeth are often displaced, they cause painful ulcers where the bit makes contact with them. Fortunately, they are easily removed. Since the horse's upper jaw is wider than his lower jaw, the upper arcade of teeth overlaps the lower, causing uneven wear in a perfectly normal mouth. As the grinding surface of the molars wear away, ridges, points and hooks remain which lacerate the tongue and the insides of the cheeks. The pressure of the bit increases the irritation. The dentist will "float" or file down the sharp edges. Caps are remnants of retained deciduous molars which become wedged between the permanent cheek teeth causing pain and uneven wear. Caps are most often seen in young horses but may be the cause of wave mouth, a pattern of uneven molar wear in older horses.

Often there will be bony prominences on the outside of the lower edge of the jaw when caps are present. Caps should be pried off before the teeth are floated.

It is essential that any dental problem be addressed immediately. If it is not attended to promptly, annoying mannerisms may become a habit and persist after the initial cause of the behavior has been removed. Further, bad teeth compromise the horse's health. If the horse's teeth cause him pain, he will not chew his food properly so that he does not get the full benefit of all that expensive hay and grain you have been feeding him. He will have a far greater tendency to experience frequent attacks of colic if his teeth are neglected. Colic is a life threatening condition. It is the leading cause of death among horses.

After eliminating discomfort as a cause of undesirable head carriage, the horse should be fitted with a standing martingale, which fastens directly to his caveson. It should be adjusted to that it does not interfere with his natural head carriage. His head should not be tied down. Pressure should be put on his nose only when he throws his head around. Do not use a running martingale (the kind in which the reins pass through a pair of rings) since the pressure to the bars of the horse's mouth can cause bruising and damage resulting in a "dead" mouth.

If your horse is sour and uncooperative he may be suffering from ulcers. It may be a smart move to run him down the road to the nearest fully equipped equine veterinary hospital and have an endoscopic exam performed to determine if this is the case. Dr. Michael Murray at the Marion duPont Scott Equine Medical Center in Leesburg, Virginia, is conducting a study of the incidence of gastric ulcers in adult horses. According to Dr. Murray, "As far as adult horses are concerned, strenuous exercise appears to be a primary factor. Racehorses have a tremendous problem with ulcers; 80% of those we have examined by endoscopy have it and it is not necessarily drug-related. Drugs like Bute and similar anti-inflammatories definitely cause ulcers, but the racehorses that don't receive Bute or other drugs also have a high rate of ulceration."

"Colic is a symptom of ulcers in only a small percentage of

cases. Horses with ulcers. . .show very subtle behavioral signs. Ulcers hurt, but we don't necessarily know that the horse is hurting, except that when you go to cinch up the girth strap the horse resents that. The horse doesn't like to train. People are having a hard time riding the horse. The horse has a very sour attitude or is a very difficult horse to handle. The reason we know that ulcers are causing that behavior is because when we successfully treat the ulcers, the behavioral changes are remarkable."[2]

In choosing a saddle, remember that it should rest on the muscles that lie on either side of the spine, not on the backbone itself. When the girth is tightened, there should be space for the width of three or four fingers to be inserted between the pommel of the saddle and the horse's withers, since the space will be diminished when the rider's weight pushes down on the saddle. If there is no space between saddle and horse, the rider's weight will rest on the spinous processes of the vertebrae which are thinly covered. Damage, thus, is inevitable: first a sore back, and then the formation of a saddle sore, sit fasts or fistulous withers. A sit fast is a hairless area of dead skin and scar tissue, due to continued pressure. These areas sometimes form fibrous attachments to the underlying bursae and ligaments of the area along which infection can travel. A fistulous withers is a deep seated abscess of the ligamentum nuchae (which runs from the poll to behind the withers and helps support the neck) and the bursae which overlie it. The infection may spread between the spinous processes of the thoracic vertebrae forming sinuses and fistulous tracts as far as the scapula with fibrous attachments to the surrounding bones and ligaments. The spinous processes may become necrotic. Often fistulas of the withers are invaded by the microorganism, Brucella, which causes Bang's disease in cattle or undulant fever (Malta fever) in man. Such infections of the withers are virtually impossible to cure by conservative measures or home remedies. Although they break open and drain, the opening usually occurs at or near the top of the withers, while the

---

[2] Dr. Michael Murray, "Veterinary Update: Stomach Ulcers in Foals and Racehorses," *Thoroughbred Times,* Lexington, Kentucky, June 1990, p. 20.

infection itself is raging several inches lower. Surgery offers the best hope of a cure, preferably performed in a complete veterinary hospital. Fistula of the withers is but another instance of a preventable injury that can get totally out of hand due to carelessness and neglect. So if your old saddle does not quite fit your new horse, replace it, or have it restuffed to fit.

Because high withers are characteristic of the Thoroughbred, and because horses in racing condition do not have their withers padded with a cushion of fat, they are particularly liable to injury and irreversible damage. Hunting saddles imported from England often are made with a high narrow tree, while German-made saddles tend to have a tree with a wider spread to fit the stout, warmblood sport horses so popular in that country. Tack stores carry saddles of various shapes and sizes and can order what they do not have in stock. There is no excuse at all for using your new horse with a saddle that does not fit him and is sure to cause him pain.

String girths made of mohair are excellent because they do not slip or chafe. Leather girths shaped around the elbow are also very good but must be cleaned after each use. If allowed to become caked with dirt, hair and dried sweat, they will soon cause a girth gall. Web girths are likely to irritate the girth area because they have a hard, abrasive edge. Never put a girth on a dirty horse or a dirty girth on a clean horse. To do so is to invite a girth sore to develop. Hose off the sweat after each ride and groom your horse thoroughly before riding. Keep your girths clean (the string ones can go in the washing machine, gentle cycle, warm water and Woolite^R; hang to dry in the sunshine) and you should have no problem in the girth area. The use of a sheepskin or artificial fleece girth cover will minimize irritation to the girth area. Needless to say, it also must be kept clean.

It is always wise to work your horse with someone around to help you, rather than working alone. This practice is both safer and more convenient and is especially important in the early phases of your horse's reschooling. In backing, or mounting your new horse for the first time, remember that at the racetrack, an exercise rider or a jockey was given a leg up on the horse, coming down as light as a feather on the saddle. No withers-pinching twisting of the saddle, or toe gouging into his side as too often happens when the horse is mounted from the ground. In getting on your former racehorse for the first time, get a leg up from someone who also holds the horse's reins. If you are not proficient at receiving a leg up, practice on a calm horse until you are, before attempting the procedure with your new horse. Or you can stand on a mounting block - an overturned metal or plastic bucket will do (a rubber bucket will collapse under your weight) - to avoid the unfamiliar and unpleasant pressure of the saddle on the horse's withers; have your assistant hold the horse and also the stirrup leather on the off side so the saddle does not twist. If your horse is reluctant to stand, have the assistant slip a slice of apple or other treat into the horse's mouth so he will learn to associate your mounting with a pleasant experience and will learn to stand quietly. If he is reluctant to stand outside, go in the barn. If he does not want to stand in the barn aisle, go into the stall, provided that the ceiling of the stall is of ample height so that you will not bump your head should he stand on his hind legs. Practice getting on and off repeatedly until it is old hat to him and he is thoroughly calm about it.

When riding the horse for the first time, it is a wise precaution to ride him in a small enclosure, such as a stoutly fenced corral or paddock, round pen or indoor arena. In a small area, he will be much less likely to bolt or to misbehave than he would in the open; should he unseat you, he will be unable to get away, injure himself or do any other sort of mischief. The rider should wear leather boots and a protective helmet of the type with a chin harness that is approved by the U.S. Pony Club.

Begin with slow work, lots of walking, turns, circles, serpentines, halts and half halts. All the early activities should tend toward calmness. Talk to him, pat him and praise him when he does well. Do not keep working him until he becomes bored. Stop while you are ahead--when he is responding cheerfully to what you ask of him. Remember that several short lessons are preferable to one long one.

Because jockeys and exercise riders use very short stirrups, they cannot use their legs in guiding the horse. Therefore, the leg aids will be new to your ex-racehorse, even though he is well broken and thoroughly bridle wise. Be tactful, be consistent and let him know when he has done the right thing.

Do not introduce something new at the beginning of a lesson. Run briefly through what the horse knows well before taking up the next step. If resistance is encountered, go back to an earlier level rather than getting in a fight with him. A fight is pointless. It leaves both horse and rider feeling cross and frustrated. The rider can only come off second best in a contest of strength. You, however, are supposed to be smarter than the horse, so use your supposedly superior intelligence to make learning a pleasant experience for him. If you do, he will learn quickly and will enjoy pleasing you. A horse resists because he does not understand, because he is uncomfortable, because the foundation for the next step has not been laid adequately, or because he is bored from too long a training session.

In general, the rider's hands control the horse's forehand (the part of him in front of the girth) while the rider's legs control the hind-quarters. Actually, the rider does not control the horse. He communicates his wishes to the horse through a consistent combination of signals known as aids. The natural aids are legs, hands, voice and weight or seat. The artificial aids are whips, spurs, martingales and side reins. The aids are employed together, in harmony, to produce the desired response from the horse. Once the aid is learned by the horse, the rider need ask him with only the lightest feel of the leg or rein and the slightest movement of his weight. Care should be taken never to give conflicting or contradictory aids, for such misuse of the aids will make the horse confused and sour. For example do not squeeze him forward by using your legs while restraining him with your hands unless you want him to back up. Do not continue to post when asking him to pick up a canter.

As the horse walks, his head nods up and down. When the rider wishes him to continue walking straight ahead at the same speed, he rewards him with a following hand that gives with the natural motion of the horse's head. In a passive, or following hand, the reins lie lightly across the rider's fingers; the reins form a straight line from the rider's elbow to the horse's mouth, maintaining light contact at all times. The hand becomes active, putting pressure on the bit, when it is closed with a gradual gesture such as the motion used in squeezing a sponge. To turn the horse to the right, the rider squeezes with the right hand while yielding slightly with the left hand so the horse can turn his head by bending his neck; at the same time he uses his right leg, squeezing with the inside of his lower leg to bend the horse using his left leg behind the girth to prevent the hindquarters from swinging out. In halting, the rider arches his back, applies even pressure with both legs and closes both hands, thus moving the horse up into a resisting hand, telling him to stop. The same aids are used in asking him to back, although he may be allowed first to take a couple of forward steps.

Bending exercises make the horse supple and responsive and also have a calming effect. Straight ahead motion is exciting, while turns tend to settle him.

Just as people have a dominant side, so do horses. Most people are right dominant while most horses are left dominant. Since most people are right handed, they usually lead the horse from their right which is his left. Further, since racing in the United States is counter clockwise and he is also led around the shed row to the left, the left handed tendency is reinforced. Therefore, the retired racehorse will flex more readily to the left. It is a common fallacy that racehorses never use their right lead because they go round to the left in a race in the U.S. and while training. If a horse cannot switch leads on the straight, he will surely be beaten. He is schooled at the track to use both leads because running all the way on one lead would tire him out so that he would have nothing left at the finish where his efforts count the most. It is just as if you were carrying a heavy suitcase or bucket of water. When one arm becomes too tired to continue, you switch the burden to the other hand. A very tired horse will switch leads repeatedly as he comes down the home stretch, trying to ease his fatigue. When starting out in reschooling your horse, make allowances for the fact that he will bend less readily to the right. If the horse seems not to understand, or resists making circles to the right, it is usually helpful to include a corner of the paddock, riding ring or indoor arena into the circle. In making the volte (small circle of 6 meters or 20 feet in diameter) use the aids, as in turning.

After a couple of calm, obedient sessions at the walk, the jog or slow, sitting trot can be introduced. It is useful in developing calmness in the horse. Voltes, serpentines, two tracking, turns on the forehand, and turns on the haunches are also excellent exercises for developing calmness, suppleness, confidence and understanding in the horse. These are the basic manège (riding school) movements of dressage and are the basis for all future training.

At the ordinary, or working trot, the horse moves forward freely with a close contact, but without restraint. The gait should be balanced and rhythmical, with good impulsion, cadence and engagement of the hindquarters. The hind feet step in the hoofprints of the front feet. This is the trot to be used for getting from one place to another. The rider rises to the trot (posts). When riding on a road or trail, rather than the confines of a ring, he should change diagonals from time to time, rather than always posting on the same diagonal, a practice which is tiring to the horse and, further, tends to make him one sided. Most horses have a preferred diagonal, whether from a natural lateral dominence, or from being ridden principally on only one diagonal, it is not certain. When you post on the diagonal he likes less well, he may put in a quick half step to shift you back to where he is more comfortable. Therefore, keep checking to make sure you are posting equally on both diagonals.

Make all of your early schooling very low key. Ask for new steps in very gradual increments. If you remain relaxed, your horse will do the same. Make haste slowly. Err on the side of caution. Never do anything to cause your horse to distrust you. Although he has the potential to become a champion, the road to success is often a circuitous one with many detours ahead. But remember, each journey begins with a single step, no matter how small. Initially, settle for a good attitude; if you can maintain that, all other things will fall into place.

The horse must learn to extend his trot. The rhythm of the

gait is not increased, but the stride is lengthened so that he covers more ground. The speed is increased due to longer step per stride rather than increasing the number of steps.

If the horse resists the bit by boring, or by raising his head, he may benefit by standing reins or being longed in a biting rig before each riding session. Side reins can be improvised from two pieces of bailing twine which are attached to the bit and to the rings on a harness back pad or to the D's on the saddle. If the saddle has no D's, the twine can be attached to the billets or to the run up stirrup irons. The side reins are adjusted so that very slight pressure is put on the horse's mouth when it is held in the usual position. Care should be taken that the pressure is not excessive and is equal on both sides. The horse relieves the pressure by flexing at the poll. Avoid too much flexion at first, gradually shortening the string over a period of time. The horse's head should not pass the perpendicular when he flexes.

Teach the canter in the riding ring. The canter is, in a sense, an artificial gait in that it is a slow, collected gallop. At liberty, a horse will trot until he can trot no faster, then break into a gallop. He will learn the canter from the sitting trot; later, he will learn to pick up the gait from a walk and later still from the halt and rein back. Although the former racehorse is already proficient at the gallop, it is not likely that he has had much experience at a canter. He will wish to drop back to a trot when first asked to canter slowly. Work him in circles, in both directions, using legs and seat to push him up under himself while maintaining light and following contact with his mouth thus helping him achieve lightness and collection.

The first time you ask him to gallop (having taught him to canter in your training ring) head him away from home to negate the gravitational pull of the barn. Begin after the horse has been ridden long enough so that the edge is off him. Do not ask for a gallop when he is feeling very fresh or when the wind is whipping up excitement all about.

While the gallop excites and stimulates the horse, the trot calms him. There is no better way to take the edge off a fresh horse than to ride him a couple of miles at a brisk trot. There is far less risk of his injuring himself at the trot than at the gallop because his weight is always supported by two legs, rather than one, as it is at certain phases of the gallop. For the horse that frets continually, a lot of trotting is the solution.

Especially during the early reschooling period, it is important that only one person ride the horse. No two riders, even though equally skilled, give the aids in exactly the same manner, just as the handwriting of two people is not identical, even though they both learned to write in the same classroom. Because riders give the aids in a slightly different manner, the horse will become confused at a time when he has a great many new things to learn. It is because of such constant confusion that livery stable mounts deteriorate as rapidly as they do; ridden by anyone and everyone, they develop all sorts of evasions as protection against further abuse by unskilled riders, becoming insensitive to the aids, even when correctly given.

Opinion is divided among trainers as to the merit of voice commands and of the feeding of treats. Horsemen are an opinionated lot and on any given subject one is likely to get widely divergent viewpoints from equally qualified spokesmen. You will hear that hand feeding is deplorable, the mark of a rank amateur and the quickest way to spoil a horse, while additionally encouraging him to bite. You will also hear that the dancing white stallions of Vienna's famous Spanish Riding School dote upon their daily sugar lumps as does a famous racing star.

The gratuitous feeding of treats is a harmful practice. Don't confuse the greedy whinny of your horse with love. Horses which are fed treats, simply for the sake of feeding treats soon become pests; like spoiled dogs who are fed tidbits from their master's plate at the table and are a nuisance at every meal. Horses that expect a treat whenever they see a person, may nip when they are disappointed.

A small lump of sugar, or better, a slice of apple or carrot, as a reward for a job well done can be a valuable training aid. Many horses are uncooperative about standing to be mounted. Refusal to stand is dangerous as well as inconvenient. If the horse is fed a treat while the rider mounts, he will soon learn to associate standing with something pleasant. The horse which is difficult to catch in the pasture can almost always be won over by giving a handout. The treat need not be continued indefinitely, but it is a great help in getting over many sticky spots. The harm, therefore, or the merit in feeding treats, depends upon the spirit in which it is given; the horse certainly knows the difference and respects the rider accordingly.

In the author's experience, voice commands are valuable training aids. Although the horse can understand only a few words, rather than long sentences, talking to him is soothing and reassuring. It is helpful for him to know the meaning of simple commands such as, "whoa," "come," "no," "walk," "trot," "canter," "back," "over," and "good boy". The use of voice commands in company is considered to be bad manners because another rider's horse may think the command is meant for him. Therefore, the use of the voice should be restricted to schooling.

If you feel that you are not sufficiently skilled to carry through on your own, by all means get help. You can ask the person who taught you to ride, if you feel confident with him. Or get in touch with a trainer whose pupils, both human and equine, are placing well at local shows. Many such professionals will come to your barn and work with you in your own familiar surroundings. Or you can have your horse vanned or trailered to his arena or training barn to take individual or group lessons. The interaction with other horses and riders is a good stimulant to improving your skills. Often what the riding master says to his other pupils will have as much relevance to your own problems as the remarks he directs at you.

Radishes and Mint Shows His Form Over Fences

Radishes and Mint (Time Tested-Plumb Dangerous by *Tudor Grey) a 16:2 hand gray stallion, in 27 starts won 6 races, was 8 times second and 3 times third for earnings of $54,640. He is a half- brother to multiple stakes winner Dangerous Leader. A tribute to Radishes and Mint's wonderful disposition and his rider's skill is his ability to combine an active stud career with success in the show ring. He is siring offspring with his "athletic prowess and excellent temperament.. he's the classic American Thoroughbred and a very special friend," according to his owner Gina Johnson of Sylvan Oaks Farm, Clearwater, Florida. (Photo courtesy of James Leslie Parker)

Chapter 12

Trail Riding

When the horse is calm, obedient and responsive at a walk, jog and trot, he is ready for slow road or trail work of an unchallenging nature. As in taking up any major new step forward in the horse's training, choose a calm day for his first outing. The horse should be accompanied by a relaxed, well mannered horse who is not likely to become frightened or to misbehave under any unusual or unforeseen circumstances. The former racehorse is used to going and coming from the track with a cold blooded stable "pony" and will readily fall in with this procedure. Remember that your Thoroughbred will take his cue as to how to behave in unfamiliar situations by observing his companion's behavior; therefore it is imperative that his role model be a dependable one.

In starting out, it is best to ride down a protected, rather narrow lane. Lock the dogs up; you don't want them flushing a deer, quail or rabbit to add excitement and confusion to what you hope will be an uneventful ride. A long straightaway of country road looks too much like the racing strip at the track and should be avoided. It is best to avoid all vehicular traffic; although the racehorse is used to seeing cars, trucks, vans and so forth, something in the ditch might cause him to shy into the path of a car. Road graders, haying equipment and cherry pickers use even lightly travelled country roads. The sight of them can unsettle the most settled mind. So, avoid public roads. Wide open spaces offer an invitation to run and should be avoided at first. Riding the horse in the pasture in which he is usually at liberty should also be avoided. Because he has been free to go where he chooses in it, he will have definite notions about where it is desirable to go. You want his first outing to be pleasant and stress free for both you and your new horse, so think ahead to avoid potentially stress producing situations.

The trail chosen for the first rides should be fairly level, as well as private, because the horse's experience has been on the level surface of the racetrack. He will find hills difficult to negotiate, especially when descending, and may refuse to move on if he is faced with a steep hill too soon. Gradually work up to riding over more rugged and challenging terrain.

Expect to meet with some reluctance when crossing streams and bridges for the first time. In teaching your Thoroughbred to go through potentially frightening situations, the calm, well-schooled horse acting as "pony" is invaluable. Many rides are spoiled because a horse balks at a wet spot, so that the rider must turn back. Therefore, learning to ford streams is a part of the trail horse's or field hunter's basic education. Make certain that the first stream you ask him to cross has a firm rock or gravel bottom; avoid crossings where there is a sticky, muddy bottom. Horses have an innate fear of marshes and wet spots in which they lose their mobility and become trapped. Flight has always been the horse's best means of survival, so it goes against his deep seated instinct to put his freedom to escape in jeopardy.

Let your former racehorse see his companion walk calmly into the water. Close your legs firmly and ask him to move on as if it were the most natural thing in the world to do. Stay relaxed yourself; nervousness on the part of the rider immediately transfers to the horse. Let him watch the well-schooled horse as he enjoys the water, pawing and snorting in it and probably taking a drink. Let your horse smell the water, approaching it slowly. If he still refuses, dismount, run up the stirrup irons, take the reins over his head and lead him, standing well to one side, so should he jump, he will not land on top of you. Let him take his time in deciding to come. Encourage him with pats and soft words. You can splash a little water on him to show him there is nothing to fear. Never get after him with a stick or otherwise abuse him since this will only reinforce his distrust of stream crossings. If he will not cross on the first attempt, come back the next day, and the day after that, if necessary. Then once he has crossed, lead him back and forth across several times with extravagant praise. After he is thoroughly willing to be led across, mount up and ride him back and forth several times. Do not be surprised if you need to repeat the whole procedure at the next stream, although not so much time will be necessary. After he has become thoroughly familiar with the trails he must learn to take his turn leading as well as following.

All the early trail work should be at a walk, gradually increasing the pace to a slow trot. It is natural for the horse to jog down a slope, accelerating to a trot by the time he reaches the bottom of the hill, then to gallop up the opposite slope. He should be discouraged from trotting down hill by using your back as you do in the halt or rein back, to slow his forward motion. In walking up a hill, rise in the stirrups to make your weight easier for the horse to carry; should he begin to trot up the hill, cease the reward of standing in your irons, use your weight against him by sitting in the saddle, only rising when he has come back to the walk. He will soon get the point. Later he will be asked to trot and gallop up hills, exercises which are excellent to develop wind and stamina, but in the early stages, he must learn to walk unless asked to do otherwise.

It is a mistake to begin to canter or gallop too early in the schooling period, although there will be every inducement to do so. The canter is an exciting gait that slips easily into a gallop and then into a dead run, which is what the horse's previous conditioning has led him to believe is expected of him. Beware the temptation to let him have a good run "to get it out of his system." The exact opposite will be the result. The horse will be fired up, rather than calmed down by the experience. For the same reason, turn down any challenge to see who has the fastest horse. The outcome can be disastrous to horses, riders and innocent bystanders. At the racetrack, every precaution is taken for safety: the racing surface is meticulously cared for; no one is allowed on the track without protective headgear; only licensed riders are allowed on the track; spectators are separated from the racetrack by stout fences and security guards; an ambulance with trained attendants is always on duty when the track is in use; unruly horses are barred from competition. Despite all the safeguards, serious injuries do occur as well as an occasional fatality. Compare the controlled environment at the racetrack with the rutted, muddy lane, rock strewn road or meadow dotted with woodchuck holes where impromptu matches are held and you will readily agree that backyard horse racing is lethal! The whole idea of reschooling is to help the horse forget entirely about being that sort of hero.

Jigging, which is an irregular, ill cadenced walk, is a symptom of nervous anxiety. The horse may either star gaze or over flex to avoid the bit while he contorts himself into a tight frame and jiggles uncomfortably (for himself as well as the rider) along. Make certain his equipment is suitable and properly fitted. Could the saddle pad be wrinkled or the girth or a billet twisted? Is the bit too severe or is the mouth piece too narrow so that his lips are pinched? To overcome the habit, the horse should be gently restrained, then rewarded with a pat, kind word and following hand as soon as he has come back to a walk. Repeat the word, "walk." Then ride him, as long as he continues a good, flat footed walk, with somewhat less contact. The halts and half halts practiced during the early training will be very helpful here. If he only jigs going toward the barn, turning him away from the barn until he stops jigging and walks quietly with his head and neck extended will be helpful. Repeat as necessary. He will soon learn what is expected of him and that he will get home more quickly by obeying than by resisting and by walking rather than jigging. Once jigging becomes a habit, it is difficult to overcome. Much patience is required. Make certain that you are not making him nervous by being tense when you ride him. If you have had a perfectly rotten day at work or school and are feeling cross, better skip the ride; horses are so very sensitive to our moods that he will surely pick up the fact that you are in a twit and think you are mad at him. Even after he does a nice, relaxed walk most of the time and will hack on the buckle, he may revert to jigging when frightened or made tense by unusual circumstances, such as going out in the company of a large number of horses, when hacking over unfamiliar country or when exposed to hounds for the first time.

Trail riding is one of the most beneficial activities for both horse and rider. It is fun to go out through the woods and across the fields with your friends. It is relaxing and enjoyable for both horse and rider to ramble along in a low key manner. The horse gains muscle tone, confidence, relaxation. He feels good about himself and life in general. No matter what eventual activity you plan for him, a quiet trail ride is part of the foundation, mental and physical, which you hope to build. Further, it is always an excellent way to unwind after the rigors of a strenuous season of hunting, showing or eventing. It keeps his mind sane as it refreshes his outlook.

The Making of a Legend

Idle Dice (registered name, pedigree, racing record and foaling date not available) raced at Waterford Park (now Mountaineer Park) near Chester, West Virginia, where he was bought by Denny Lenehan, who sold him to Bernie Taurig. Taurig showed the gelding as a hunter until selling him to Rodney Jenkins of Orange, Virginia. Idle Dice and Rodney Jenkins became synonomous with Grand Prix jumping in the 1970's winning at least 15 Grand Prix events, including the President's Cup at Washington in 1971 and 1972 and the American Gold Cup in 1973, 1974 and 1975. He jumped 7'2" to win the Puissance in 1972. The last major victory was the $25,000 Mercedes "I Love New York" Grand Prix in 1981. He was officially retired at the Gold Cup in 1985 with earnings of $125,000.[1] When Idle Dice was at his best, no horse could beat his combination of jumping skill and speed. "Jenkins once said of him, 'I'd go there and almost know if I wanted to win I probably could. He was a super horse.'"[2] Jenkins says that he prefers the Thoroughbred to other breeds of horse and finds no problem in training retired racehorses.[3]

---

[1] John Strassberger, *loc. cit.*
[2] *Ibid.*
[3] Rodney Jenkins, Orange, Virginia, Telephone Conversation, June 1990.

Chapter 13

Teaching Him to Jump

In teaching your retired racehorse to jump, consideration must first be given to his age. Although he can be longed over a low obstacle at three, he should be at least four years old, by the calendar, not by the rule book, before he is asked to carry a rider over a fence. If he has had any major unsoundness, such as a bowed tendon, at least a full year should elapse between his retirement and beginning to learn to jump.

Many former racehorses with legs bearing the evidence of previous inflammatory conditions have gone on to make a successful career over fences after a sufficient interval of rest. Roger Boltz's gifted horse, Creche, who had a large osselet, was shown extensively in working hunter, junior hunter, equitation and jumper classes; a separate room was needed to house the trophies he had won. During the same period, he was hunted regularly with the Lauray Hunt of Bath, Ohio. Shagwrack's bowed tendon did not hinder him in jumping five feet in a bold and brilliant manner and competing in Pony Club rallies and other combined training events for Shelly Emory. Whatitoldyou, a winner at major tracks - Hialeah, Belmont, Aqueduct and Santa Anita - placed in major stakes while earning almost $90,000, had ringbone and a great deal of scar tissue in his tendon sheaths. He was successfully shown and hunted by Dana Baker of Solon, Ohio. Three Grand, winner of 14 races from two to nine, acquired a big ankle that bothered him not at all; he was a safe and consistent jumper. He pony clubbed with Bridget Bills of Bath, Ohio.

The horse's temperament is another factor to be considered before teaching the horse to jump. Like galloping, jumping is an exciting activity and should be taken up only after the horse is hacking quietly. The preliminary steps, however, may be begun quite early in the horse's retraining and will help keep him from becoming bored.

After the basic ring maneuvers, work over cavalletti is the first step in teaching the horse to jump. Cavalletti develop the horse's balance, agility and coordination. They are helpful in making him supple, calm and obedient. The horse learns to place his feet with precision and gains greater impulsion and engagement of the hindquarters. Cavalletti are also used to teach the horse to extend or to shorten his stride.

Begin with one simple, rounded pole 10 to 12 feet long lying on the ground. Let the horse walk over it. He may want to walk around it. If he does, place one end at a 90° angle against the fence or wall of the arena and another pole parallel to the wall or fence and about 4 feet from it. Squeeze him on firmly with your legs, patting him and telling him he is a "good boy" when he obeys. He may trip or rap his ankle the first try, but on the next pass he will pay better attention. Walk over the pole from both directions. When he is walking calmly and carefully over a single pole, another may be added parallel to and about four or five feet from the first, the actual distance to be determined by the size of the horse and the length of his stride. Choose a distance that seems comfortable and natural to him. Gradually add poles at regular intervals until he can negotiate a series of six or eight without touching one. The length of time it takes to progress from one pole to a series depends upon the skill of the rider and the attitude of the horse - anywhere from 15 minutes to a week and a half.

When he has become quite used to walking over a series of poles, let him trot over the last pole. If he finds that to be awkward, go back to the single pole and trot over it; then proceeding as before, adding more poles, one at a time, until he can trot over a series without stepping on one. Be careful not to look down at the poles, but to look ahead; you should rise in the stirrups as you would at a trot, but not post, while maintaining a quiet hand and light contact with the horse's mouth. At a trot, the horse's head does not move up and down as it does at a walk or gallop. If you look down, the horse will feel the shift in your weight and think he is meant to stop, so always look where you are going.

Graduating from the simple poles laid on the ground, set up a variable height cavalletti, which can easily be made by nailing a ten foot pole to an X-shaped 3' x 3' support. The height of the pole, then, can be varied from 10" to 19" by how the X is turned. Although the pole can be made from a square piece of lumber as it comes from the builder's supply, it is better to have a rounded rail so as to be less likely to scar the horse's legs if he makes a misstep. Quite acceptable poles can be made from the trunks of small, straight trees. Start by walking the horse over the cavalletti set at the lowest height. At this stage you may have to go back to the single element on the ground, adding additional cavalletti, evenly spaced, as he gains confidence.

When the horse can trot over a series of six or more cavalletti in good style, having progressed from the 10" to the 15" height over a series of calm and gradual sessions, remove the next to last cavalletti and turn the last to 19" so that he will give a little hop to get over it. The difficulty of the first little jump can be increased by putting a cavalletti at the 15' height immediately in front of the last one at 19". The stair step effect of the two makes an inviting obstacle. The challenge of the jump can be increased by widening the width between its two elements. Gradually the obstacles can be arranged so that the horse canters over two, then three cavalletti at the 19" height. All three may be piled on top of each other to make a 3'3" jump. The versatility of cavalletti is limited only by your imagination and ingenuity.

The time it takes to advance from one step to another varies greatly from horse to horse. Much depends upon the horse's temperament, his degree of coordination and most of all, upon his mental outlook and, of course, upon the skill and tact of the rider. If you get left behind, jab the horse in the mouth and plop down hard in the saddle, your horse will soon become discouraged, because, in effect, he is being punished, rather

Trotting over cavaletti develops balance, impulsion and collection

Note how the rider can loop a finger into the neck strap to maintain his balance over a fence without catching the horse in the mouth.

than rewarded when he jumps. A stirrup leather fastened around the horse's neck into which you can loop a finger, will give you additional stability and prevent your inadvertently snatching your horse's mouth. It is no disgrace to use a neck strap or to grab mane, but it is a disgrace to abuse the horse's mouth and to punish him for doing what you asked of him. Trust is the essential element in reschooling. If you and your horse are in mutual harmony and accord you can accomplish a great deal with him, even though your skills may not be of the highest level.

As in all things where horses are concerned, it is best to progress slowly. There is no surer way to establish resistance than by over-facing your horse, that is by asking more of him than he is ready to give.

Your new horse should not be schooled over jumps more often than twice a week. It is important that he not be allowed to become bored. Vary the routine. Hack him out over new trails in addition to ring work in which voltes, leg yields, turns on the forehand, two-trackings, turns on the haunches and other suppling exercises are practiced.

Do not keep your horse at one exercise or jumping over one obstacle until he becomes sour and begins to think up evasive actions. Always let the session end on a pleasant note with the horse being rewarded and praised for a good effort.

If your horse is very keen, jumping over a series of obstacles will tend to excite him. He may get "hot" on a straight course where there are several fences in a row. Changes of direction, on the other hand, tend to calm him and to steady him as he thinks about what he is expected to do next, rather than rushing heedlessly ahead.

If he is getting too hot over fences, do not jump on each approach to a fence. Trot him past it, or halt in front of it, circle the fence and go on.

In teaching the horse to jump more challenging obstacles, the ground line must be considered. Because of the horse's very limited binocular vision, he judges his approach by looking at the part of the barrier nearest the ground. For this reason, he is more likely to jump cleanly and willingly over a solid, substantial obstacle, than he is over a flimsy one. In jumping a rail, lay a pole on the ground on the approach to the fence as far from the bottom of the fence as the top is from the ground. The ground line will help guide the horse in taking off for the jump. It will also encourage him not to pop his fences, but to stand back from them and develop scope in jumping. Pine boughs can be piled in front of a rail to make it appear more inviting.

A homemade jump course can be easily improvised. It should offer as wide a variety as possible of both natural and artificial obstacles: bales of hay or straw, old telephone poles, a chicken coop, or a simulated stone wall. A realistic looking "brick wall" can be made by applying masking tape in a brick pattern on a plywood panel, painting it red and then removing the tape. Anticipate the type of obstacle he is likely to see in the show ring, then duplicate it at home.

Hunter fences are basically natural obstacles to simulate those found in hunting country: post and rails, brush, stone wall, white board fence or gate, chicken coop, hedge and oxer; while targets and striped rails are prohibited.

Jumper courses are more likely to offer bizarre obstacles such as targets, brick walls, striped poles, and barrels painted with various designs and a "road closed" barrier, as well as more conventional appearing fences. A water jump is also likely to be included. Often potted plants are placed in front of the jumps.

Include as many different things as you can think of on your practice course. It is far cheaper to do your schooling at home than in the ring at a show. If he will jump over targets and striped barrels when they are part of low schooling fences, he will not be frightened by them when seeing them on a jumper course at his first show. In asking for increased effort from the horse, it is preferable to increase the spread rather than the height of the fence. Schooling jumps need not be higher than 3 feet or three feet, six inches. The horse who will jump three feet cleanly in his home ring will fly over anything up to four feet in the hunt field or show ring.

When constructing your schooling jumps, never construct a chicken coop from two pieces of plywood, hinged at the top. If a horse hits such an obstacle, it folds up, becoming several inches taller than when its sides are spread out to make a bottomless triangle. A simple rap or touch can thus be translated into a dangerous fall. Make your coop a stable, three-sided obstacle, or lean a single 4' x 8' panel of plywood against a rail to simulate a coop.

Opinion is divided in regard to the use of wings. Many authorities consider them to be indispensable in the early stages of training to prevent run outs, while other authorities, equally eminent, feel that wings are an unnecessary crutch and that, if the preliminaries have been carefully observed, there is no need for them. A horse who will jump over fences without wings will jump over fences with wings, although the reverse is not always true. So suit yourself; use whichever method works best for you.

11 Seasons at the Top

Kwe-We (Interpretation-Gold Loma by *Brig O'Doon) was foaled in Nevada in 1955. As a racehorse, he was once second and twice third in 17 starts at two and three. Renamed San Lucas, his career as a jumper is legendary. The 17:3 hand gelding's international career spanned eleven seasons under USET rider Frank Chapot. The pair competed in 43 Nations Cups of which the USET won 26 and placed second in 12. He won 36 international classes. He was a member of the gold medal winning team at the Pan American Games in 1963, and the silver medal team in 1967. Few horses remain at the top of the game for so long a time span, but this unfashionably bred gelding was truly a world-class performer. San Luas with Frank Chapot up (far right) is shown here with the American Team after winning the Prix des Nations in 1972. (Photo courtesy of Freudy Photo)

Chapter 14

Going to Shows

In showing your horse for the first time, begin with a small local schooling show, preferably one to which you can hack. Ride around the grounds to let the horse get used to the noise and excitement. If schooling is allowed in the ring at any time, take advantage of the opportunity. If he seems nervous and upset you will be wise not to enter him. All the activity, strange horses, crowd and public address system may make him think he is back at the races, not to mention the fact that you may be feeling pretty tense and up tight yourself. Perhaps your vet will tranquilize him for the first ride around the show ground, so that having seen it all while remaining calm, he will remember in tranquility the nice outing you and he had at the show grounds. You may have to repeat this procedure more than once before you both feel calm and confident enough to actually enter a class. Do not enter your horse in a class if he has been tranquilized. To do so is in violation of AHSA rules as well as all canons of good sportsmanship. Horses are randomly blood tested for forbidden substances at AHSA affiliated shows. Spare yourself the potential embarrassment, fine and penalties.

Before planning to show, familiarize yourself with the current American Horse Shows Association Rule Book. The rules are modified from year to year so if you are not referring to the most recent edition, you are not playing with a full deck of cards. It would be a pity to have a good performance nullified or to risk elimination for an infringement of the rules, such as appearing in a flat class using a martingale.

Traditionally, hunters are presented with braided manes and tails, although at small, informal schooling shows braiding is not usually necessary. Snaffles, pelhams or full bridles may be used; nose bands are required. Any unusual type of noseband or bit may, at the discretion of the judge, be discriminated against. The use of crops, bats and unroweled spurs is optional. A hard hat is mandatory in jumping classes.

The hunter division is separated into breeding, green and working classifications. The breeding classes which are shown in hand are judged on conformation, quality, substance and suitability to become, or, in the case of mares and stallions, to produce horses suitable to the hunt field. Classes are further divided into green (first and second years of showing) and working or regular (not restricted by previous showing), Thoroughbred and non-Thoroughbred, small (15:2-1/2 hands or under), lightweight (rider under 165 lbs.) middleweight (to 185 lbs.) and heavyweight (up to 205), amateur, amateur owner, qualified (hunted with recognized hunt) and corinthian (ridden by amateur who is member of recognized hunt in hunting attire) and side saddle. Other classifications include ladies, maiden, novice, limit, young hunters, pairs, teams and so on.

Thoroughbreds excel at jumping and dressage. With their easy, correct, ground covering gaits they are natural candidates for road hack and open English Pleasure classes. If the judge is American Saddle Horse oriented, however, he may prefer a horse with higher action than the Thoroughbred.

Stock horse type is specified in the rule book in the Western Division. Most Thoroughbreds are not sufficiently compact to be looked upon with favor in western classes. They are too likely to become fired up under contest conditions to do well in the western timed events such as barrel racing. There have been exceptions. Wisp O'Dew (Heathermore-Scamper Lass), a Thoroughbred, was an accomplished cutting horse, owned by the E. M. Kulver Cattle Ranch of Montana. Beverly Blue (Gay Town-Medina Blue by King's Blue) was used in flag and barrel racing before becoming a broodmare.

Through the years, Thoroughbreds have placed well in

competitive trail rides beginning with the first Green Mountain Horse Association 100 Mile Ride in 1936, won by the retired race mare Town Gossip (Bunga Buck-Twinola). In 1937, a Thoroughbred was second in the 100 Mile Ride. In 1965, Nike, a Thoroughbred owned and ridden by Ann Gill of Barant, Vermont, won the 100 Mile Ride. In 1990, the grand champion of the Vermont 100 Mile Trail Ride was Bangkok, (Lord Tomboy out of My Jeanie Gal by Mon Easy) owned and ridden by Steve Rojek of South Woodstock, Vermont. The black gelding was the first Thoroughbred to win the ride since 1977, when Steve also won riding the mare Perkion by Perion Land, a grandson of Hyperion and out of Tuffy Girl by Rhodes Scholar.

In general, whatever a Thoroughbred sets out to do, he does to the utmost, whether running a race, following hounds, jumping grand prix fences or, unfortunately if he decides to become an outlaw, becoming a thoroughly bad one. According to Michael Clayton "it is. . .perfectly true that there is nothing a common horse can do that a Thoroughbred cannot do better."[1] The only thing he cannot do is tolerate rough handling. Since he is more intelligent than the common horse, he learns more quickly, but he is also more sensitive so be careful what you teach him.

[1] Michael Clayton, *The Chase,* Stanley Paul, London, 1987, p 85.

CHAMPERTY

Champerty, a modest winner on the flat found his forte in steeplechasing. Winner of 32 of 37 starts over timber in seven states over eighteen different courses, he set two new course records. He was the National Hunt Race Association Timber Horse of the Year. Champerty was retired from steeplechasing to be a staff horse in the hunt field and family pet. (Photos courtesy Randy Waterman.)

Chapter 15

Some Success Stories

Included throughout this book are examples of former racehorses which have gone on to new careers after leaving the racetrack. A common thread runs through all these case histories. That common thread is not pedigree - which runs the gamut from illustrious to obscure. Nor is it length of stay at the track; that factor varies from a few months to several years and more than 100 starts. It certainly is not racetrack performance which varies from unraced to being a stakes winner.

In every instance there is a bond of trust and respect between horse and rider so that their joint efforts are truly a partnership based on mutual dependence and affection. The horses are described by their owners as "a member of the family," and "my best friend." Like faithful dogs, they know their names and come when called. They are further described as "bold," "brave" and "courageous" when facing obstacles that would daunt an ordinary horse or when overcoming potentially life threatening illness or injury. A high degree of intelligence coupled with great innate ability as well as their willing spirit and fluid gaits are other characteristics consistently mentioned by the owners of the above Thoroughbreds.

After rapport between horse and rider was established, each horse was brought along slowly and sensibly, progressing from easy lessons to more advanced work. The riders are both amateur and professional, of divergent levels of ability, yet all achieved gratifying results at the level of performance wished, from quiet trail riding to Grand Prix jumping, and the upper levels of dressage and combined training.

Truly, anything an ordinary horse can do, a Thoroughbred can do better. What follows here are but a few examples.

US Park Service Police

When describing the horses used in the United States Park Police Horsemounted Unit, Officer Ron Markland states, "Most have come off the racetrack. Of the current group of 22 new mounts at the training center, five are of various breeds while the rest are Thoroughbreds. . .I personally like the Thoroughbreds for. . .their heart or boldness. . .I have seen them be able to tolerate a lot more than many cold blooded horses."[1]

Initially used in Rock Creek Park in Washington, D.C., a 1900 acre tract of heavily wooded, steep terrain, the mounted police demonstrated superior mobility and visibility. They are effective in areas where both officers on foot and in motor vehicles are at a disadvantage. The mounted patrols are highly effective in crowd control. A well-mannered police horse also serves as an effective public relations asset.

Horses for the mounted patrol, all of which are donated, are selected on a basis of size and soundness. The minimum height is 15:3, with 16 hands preferred. "A horse should be well-balanced, muscular, and long-legged. He must have good stamina, carriage and feet and a well-muscled back."[2]

The horses are put through a rigorous training program to accustom them to the sights and sounds they may encounter in the line of duty, such as sirens, horns, drums, gunshots, firecrackers, applause, motorcycles and other traffic noises. The police horse must learn to stand quietly while being struck with soft objects such as rags, sponges, hats and balloons. Compatability of horse and rider is stressed so that they may function as a harmonious and effective team.

Dressage is also part of the police horse's training to enhance his balance, flexibility and obedience. He learns to side-step,

---

[1] Officer Ron Markland, Letter, June, 1990.
[2] *Guideline Manual*, United States Park Police, Washington, D.C.

pass and back, useful movements in crowd control. He must also learn to jump so as to get over barriers in his path.3

Although most of the horses serving in the United States Park Service Police Horsemounted Unit are geldings, a few well-mannered Thoroughbred stallions are also used, while in some units, a few mares serve along side the geldings.

"The average length of service for police work is 10 to 15 years," according to Officer Ron Markland. These horses prove themselves to be valuable members of the force, well worth the time and effort spent in their retraining.4

Ex-Racehorse Stands Guard

Ninty per cent of the mounts in the U.S. Park Service Horsemounted Police are Throughbreds. Most are former racehorses. Officer William Good and Ardent John, a stallion, stand guard outside the White House. (Photo courtesy of the U.S. Park Service)

---

3 *Ibid*, p. 18.
4 *Ibid*, p. 12.

BOMBER (Nashlin)

Nashlin, now better known as Bomber, a 16:1 chestnut gelding, is another success story in a new life after the racetrack in which he earned a total of $72 in 9 starts at 2 and 3. But, let rider Robin Williams of Goochland, Virginia tell his tale:

"In October, 1978, Nashlin was sold off the meat wagon for 50 cents a pound to Capt. Rhett Taylor, USAF, then stationed at Barkdale AFB in Louisiana. Capt. Taylor named him 'Bomber' in reference to her career. She schooled him to jump and showed him some at the local level. Her primary focus was dressage, and she competed with him successfully through Second level. In 1984 and 1985, Capt. Taylor was stationed at Langley Field in Virginia, and a professional rider showed Bomber to the year-end championship in the Open Hunter Division of the Peninsula Horse Show Association.

"In 1985, when Capt. Taylor was transferred overseas, I took the horse as a temporary replacement for my hunting horse, who was in foal. Although Bomber had scarcely been out of the ring when I got him, he was an honest jumper and had a quiet, willing attitude, so I thought I could at least make do for a season with him. Little did I know what a wonderful hunting horse I was getting!

"I whip in to the Deep Run Hounds, and Bomber had to go to work roading hounds as soon as I got him in September. He learned about hounds in one day, which was about as long as it took him to learn anything. The second time I had him out hunting, I had to carry a hound several miles back to the truck across the front of my saddle. Bomber never flinched. Bomber jumped every trappy, funny-looking fence and crossed every steep, muddy creek in our country for five seasons. He jumped gates, fences with riders nailed over them and barbed wire with my coat laid over it. On one occasion, I tied Bomber to a tree (with my best braided reins!) and left him for 20 minutes while I pursued hounds on foot. My exercise girl, who had very little experience, learned to jump on Bomber, and he packed her in the field on numerous occasions.

"Bomber never confused the excitement of the hunting field with the more refined requirements of competition. The moment he stepped into a dressage or show ring, he instantly relaxed. A beautiful mover, he always won the hack class, in any company. He cleaned up at the Deep Run hunter trials and his name is on the championship challenge bowl twice. In 1986, at the request of the Jt-MFHs, Bomber and I represented Deep Run at the State Field Hunter Championship.

"Bomber was truly a family horse. Toddlers could groom his tummy and knees, and the most timid beginner could trail ride with confidence. He also adopted and raised the suckling-weanling of my mare, who was a very indifferent mother.

"One summer I loaned him to a friend for Pony club and he was part of a winning rally team.

"I always thought the only horses who came when called were on movie sets, but Bomber, bless him, knew his name and galloped to the gate when called!"

The failed race horse did it all, "Reschooled to excel at dressage and local hunter shows, as staff horse in hunting field, "packer" in hunting field, pony club mount, hunter trial champion, leadline pony and babysitter for weanlings."[5]

_____

[5] Robin Wiliams, Goochland, Virginia, letter April 26, 1990.

Robin Williams Aboard Bomber
(Photo Courtesy James S. Carr)

Ribotmar in a jumper class with Ran Shachelford up
(Photo Courtesy Ran Shachelford)

RIBOTMAR

Ribotmar (Blood Royal-Mar Best by Hurry to Market), a dark bay or brown gelding foaled in 1983, was big at birth and grew at an alarmingly fast rate. Sixteen hands as a yearling, he reached an astounding eighteen hands. When his knees were X-rayed for maturity, to see if epiphyseal closure was complete, Dr. Ron Genovese of Randall Veterinary Hospital said that the youngster not only had the biggest knees he had ever seen in a two-year-old, but were also the largest knees he had ever X-rayed in a horse of any age! A horse with warmblood size and substance and docile temperament, the Blood Royal (*Ribot-Nataska by Dedicate) colt did not look like a promising race prospect; he failed to sell at a yearling auction. Brought along very slowly, he did not start until late spring of his three-year-old year. Outrun in his first attempt, he came back to win his second by a widening ten lengths. He won twice more, both times in allowance company and was retired with lifetime earnings of $16,850.

Ribotmar ran over hurdles in sanctioned steeplechase races for one season without success. He was then sent to Laura Casati's stable for jumper training where he showed a lot of talent. He was purchased there by Ran Shachelford, of Roanoke, Virginia, a tall young man who was looking for a big horse to show in hunter and jumper classes. The pair has shown successfully in Virginia shows and has won a loyal following of local fans.[16]

Ran and Ribotmar qualified for the Washington National Horse Show where they had good rounds in Regular Working Hunter classes but were not in the ribbons. After the show, the big gelding was sold to David and Shannon Tripaldi of California. He is now trained and shown by Dick Widger, a professional on the West Coast Circuit. Under the new name, House of Cards, Ribotmar has continued his winning ways in this competitive area. In May of 1991, he was Regular Working Hunter Champion at the Seal of Approval show in Monterey.

---

[16] Ran Shachelford, Roanoke, Virginia, letter, May 1990.

RO BUFFALO

Ro Buffalo, a bay gelding born in 1975 (Flying Lark-Leo's Cake by Leisure Time), trained like a champion, reeling off fast works in the morning. But like a typical "morning glory," he did not live up to his advance billings and failed to run to his morning brilliance during the races. Unfortunately he fell into bad hands. To wake him up, he was zapped with an electrical device both in his stall and in the starting gate. Such a procedure is not a routine training measure. It is specifically prohibited by the rules of racing. Even the possession of an electrical device will result in severe penalty to the offender. A prominent jockey, Bennie Feliciano, was ruled off for life in the State of Illinois because the security police at Arlington Park found a device in the glove compartment of his car.

As an evasion to the abuse to which he was subjected, Ro developed the dangerous habit of flipping in the gate - rearing up and throwing himself over backwards. He was barred from organized racing, but continued to race for another year at bush meets where the horses started without a gate. In a four season career as a racehorse, Ro started 34 times, winning once, finishing second once, and third 4 times for earnings of $1,828. He retired with a thoroughly soured attitude and the knowledge that he could avoid any situation he did not like by doing his number. The young girl who bought him as a 7-year-old was terrified of him and eager to be rid of him.

Enter thirteen-year-old Tamara Maben of Madras, Oregon who was looking for a Thoroughbred dressage prospect. Darleen Maben, Tamara's mother described Ro as the skinniest horse she had ever seen. (Could someone have been trying to starve him into submission?) After he had metabolized all his stored fat, he had consumed most of his muscle tissue, as well, which animals do in the final stages of starvation. Ro was heavily infested with lice which are notorious for taking possession of severely debilitated horses. Almost hairless, he had open sores all over his body. An abscessed foot had been left untreated so that the sole of the hoof and the frog were eaten away by infection. The Mabens bought him more from pity than hope, rather than leaving him where he was to die of neglect.

Literally years were spent gaining Ro's confidence and in nursing him back to health with love and patience. His lethal tendency to flip at the mere prospect of unpleasantness was overcome through establishing rapport with him. Tamara started taking Ro to shows to get him used to things. He began winning in both English and western pleasure classes. "He just got better and better. As his confidence grew, so did his athletic ability to do anything Tamara asked him to do. . .It's a give and take relationship. . .Ro's arrogance and free spirit is why he is so elegant." Ro and Tamara have competed in dressage, English pleasure, reining, trail and versatility classes. He won the Buccaneer Memorial Trophy for All Around Champion and Most Versatile Thoroughbred Horse for 1985, 1987 and 1988. In dressage, his scores are consistently in the 60th percentile. He is ready to advance to First and Second Level. For three years he represented the Thoroughbred at the Oregon Horse-A-Fair, an all-breed exhibition, put on by the Oregon Horsemen's Association. Tender loving care accomplished what harsh, insensitive methods could not. Says Darleen Maben, "Ro Buffalo's story is special because it shows that even the worst of. . .rogues can be reconditioned to be a valuable, loving horse. . .he is still accomplishing new feats, but most of all, we love him and he loves us."[7]

---

[7] Darleen Maben, Madras, Oregon, Letter, May, 1990.

Tamara Maben and Ro Buffalo
(Photo courtesy J. Bortvedt Photography)

Noma Dene and His Mistress Mary Jo Spurgeon
(Photo Courtesy Mary Jo Spurgeon)

NOMA DENE

Noma Dene (Multnomah-Robin Rose by *Touba), a bay mare foaled in 1969, won two races at 3 and 4, earning $2,512 in 48 starts from 2 through 4. She was bought at age 11 by Mary Jo (Heitzman) Spurgeon of Colton, Oregon, who showed her briefly. The mare hated the show ring, but took to the trails with enthusiasm. Mary Jo on the faithful Noma Dene has opened up 50 miles of trail in the rugged Bureau of Land Management forests near her home on the slopes of the aptly named Goat Mountain.

"Very little of the land we have to work with is flat. Most of it is rough and steep. The trail we made up to Goat Mountain is 10 miles of a steady, rocky climb. And the way down to Clark Creek Falls clings to the side of a cliff.

"I never have to worry about Noma Dene's endurance in wind or limb or her desire. She is a worker who tackles the trails like a ballerina, with grace and style. She is an example of the ultimate trail horse. I feel very well mounted.

"She does her job well. Whether it is to wait quietly tied to a tree while I hike down a canyon to scout a route for a new trail; plough through chest high brush where there is no trail yet; hold still while I cut high limbs while mounted; or pack me into and out of a steep canyon, with her help all this work is less of a chore.

"Noma Dene continues to be my companion, as I go armed into the woods with loppers and hand saw in the never ending battle to maintain the trails we have built together. She is an example that the show ring isn't the only place a horse can prove to be a champion."[8]

The Thoroughbred Exhibitors' Association has established a perpetual endurance trophy named in honor of this gallant mare, who has become a legend in her own lifetime. At age 21, she is still going strong.

---

[8] Mary Jo (Heitzman) Spurgeon, Colton, Oregon, Letter, June, 1990.

DRESS GRAY (MR. SUNNI DUST)

The gray, 1980, Florida-bred gelding Mr. Sunni Dust (Madison Heights-Hyper Dust by Dumar) won once, as a three-year-old at Fairmount Park in Illinois. In four racing seasons with 28 lifetime starts, he earned a total of $3,303.

As a six year old, he was given to a young woman who wanted a trail horse. She asked her neighbor, Anne Weber, an accomplished horsewoman, to retrain the horse for her, which she agreed to do. At the end of the reschooling period, Harry Weber, Anne's husband, bought the gelding for her as an anniversary present, since the previous owner no longer wanted him. Renamed Dress Gray, the gelding began showing as a Pre-Green Hunter in a few winter schooling shows, then moved directly to Training Jumper. Dress Gray excelled as a jumper; his talent helped him move up the ladder of competition quickly with only a minimum of showing, due to time and financial constraints.

In 1988, Dress Gray was Champion Modified Jumper in Mason City, Iowa at the INHJA Summer Show. "The modified division, used correctly, is somewhere between intermediate and open. It gives horses trying to get to open and horses no longer eligible for the intermediate a place to go."[9]   At St. Louis National Charity Horse Show he was Reserve Champion Amateur Owner Jumper. In 1989, Dress Gray was Reserve Champion Preliminary Jumper at Mission Valley Pony Club Show, Champion Amateur Owner Jumper at Bridlespur Horse Show where he won all three classes, and Champion Junior/Amateur Owner Jumper at White Fox Manor Horse Show. He was third in the $5,000 Junior/Amateur Owner Classic at Milwaukee, where he was one of the few horses that had not done Grand Prix Competition. Tony Font rode him in the Open Division at St. Louis where he received ribbons in both classes entered. He qualified for the Zone VII Finals in Los Colinas, Texas, and won the Junior/Amateur Owner Classic

[9] George Morris, "The Making of a Grand Prix Jumper," *The Chronicle of the Horse,* Middleburg, Virginia, March 2, 1990, p. 67.

Zone VII Finals Championship, to wind up the 1989 season, as Reserve Champion Amateur Owner Champion Jumper for Zone VII.

In 1990, Anne and Dress Gray have done only one "A" show, Springtime in Dixie, at Memphis, where they were again Champion Amateur Owner Jumper and Champion Modified Jumper, winning four of six classes.

In addition to his show career, Dress Gray has foxhunted. From 1985, until April of 1990, Anne was Huntsman for the Bridlespur Hunt, until resigning when she moved to Bowling Green, Missouri. "I hunted hounds off Gray several times, and he was a delight, because he is so incredibly brave."[10]

Dress Gray and Anne Barry Weber
(Photo courtesy of Horse and Ryder)

[10] Anne Barry Weber, Bowling Green, Missouri, letter, May 21, 1990.

HARVEY (RANK'S AXE)

Rank's Axe (*The Axe II-Easy Listening by Jackal) a gray gelding foaled in 1978, started 28 times, winning twice and placing third twice. In 1985, Adrienne Deusch of Guttenberg, New Jersey bought him from Los Alamos Dressage Center, Freehold, New Jersey where he was used as a school horse. Since that time, she has competed with the beautiful and versatile Harvey in recognized dressage shows from Vermont to Virginia, placing sixth in the AHSA Zone Awards at Training Level, qualifying for Zone Finals at First Level and earning half the scores necessary of a USDF Bronze Medal. Additionally, Harvey has been started in harness by Stewart Thomson of Connecticut. He took to harness training so readily that the plan is to start showing him in Pleasure Driving classes as well. Being a natural ham, Harvey loves costume classes and no outfit is too outlandish for him to accept.

"He's a wonderful trail horse: confident, enthusiastic and sure footed, alone or with company, on the bit or on the buckle. . .I'm very, very fond of this horse. I am indeed. He's a marvelous character - and has a marvelous character (Any misconceptions or prejudices I ever had against Thoroughbreds/ex-racehorses he dismantled years ago.) He's taught me a great deal in many ways. . .What he's done best is to be a source of joy."[11]

---

[11] Adrienne Deutsch, Guttenberg, New Jersey, letter, May, 1990.

The Versatile Harvey Under Saddle and In Harness
(Top and middle photos courtesy Terri Miller.
Bottom, courtesy Stewart Thomson, trainer)

MR. HEBO

Mr. Hebo (Happy Lancer-New Assignment by Foreign Policy) a bay gelding foaled in 1963, was lightly raced for two seasons, making twenty starts of which he won two, was twice second and once third for earnings of $2,033. Until he was eighteen, he changed hands frequently, sixteen times in all. He was used as a working stock horse on a ranch in Tallamook, as an open jumper in Pebble Beach, California, competed in reining, eventing and endurance riding. He was also shown in halter and by youngsters in 4-H. He received the High Point Thoroughbred Gelding Performance Horse Award in 1978 from the Oregon Horse Association. He was also the mount for the Rodeo Queen when owned by Judy White of Salem, Oregon. He usually stayed with one owner a year or less, until he came to Teddi Taylor of Colton, Oregon. He was twice shown to High Point Championships in Trail and Western Pleasure at an age where most performers are retired. With Teddi, he had at last found a permanent home. As this book went to press, word came that he died at the age of 29. Teddi had told us, "When his end comes he will be buried on our property, as befits a champion."

Another old timer owned by Teddi Taylor is Big Day (Super Idol- Broker's Lou, by Broker's Tip) an unraced bay foaled in 1965. He has been a champion, also, in both performance and halter classes. Teddi pays him the supreme compliment, "He did everything we asked of him."[12]

As a fan of the Thoroughbred, Teddi's enthusiasm is unsurpassed. She is a true believer that Thoroughbreds can do it all. She has proved it by showing her Thoroughbreds in western classes, beating the stock horse breeds at their own game in their own backyard. "Thoroughbreds *can* do it all. (Some riders play lords and ladies and some play cowboys and Indians.) Enjoy your Thoroughbred! That's what it's all about."[13]

---

[12] Teddi Taylor, Colton, Oregon, letter, May 1990.
[13] *Ibid.*

Mr. Hebo as a Western Pleasure Horse
(Photo courtesy of Judy White-Taylor)

On the Jazz with Vicki Trout
(Photo Courtesy Fred Newman)

ON THE JAZZ (WEST JERSEY GUY)

Winner on the flat, West Jersey Guy (West Coast Scout-Mad Moll by Laugh Aloud), a bay gelding foaled in 1978, was renamed On the Jazz after Vicki Trout bought him from a New Jersey sales barn in 1983. She describes her bay 17:1-1/2 acquisition as completely green and a "handful". After training in dressage and jumping, the pair began eventing. Five friends of Vicki's started eventing at the same time she did, also on green horses. Of the five friends, three were soon left behind in Novice. Two moved on with Vicki and On the Jazz to Training Level, eventing all over New Jersey, Pennsylvania, Delaware and Maryland together. While the friends all had trouble with their horses at the more challenging obstacles at the higher level of competition, Jazz flew around the courses, not intimidated by drops and ditches that stopped her friends' horses. He qualified for the Training Level Championship. The last remaining of the five friends were left behind when Jazz and Vicki moved up to Preliminary, eventing all up and down the East Coast against the country's top three day riders. Vicki modestly credits all the success to "my very talented horse".

The same Thoroughbred courage that helped Jazz be a bold jumper also helped him overcome a serious trailer accident and a life-threatening bout with pleuritis. Both times he was called a poor risk, but overcame the odds.[14]

---

[14] Vicki Trout, Sierra Vista, Arizona, letter, May 1990.

*Puncheon II shows his Champion Hunter form.

The imported Thoroughbred gelding *Puncheon II (Punchinello-Bridge of Clyde by Falls of Clyde), a 16:1 hand bay, raced for three seasons in the United States. Starting 29 times, he won twice and placed second twice. His racing ended with slab fractures in both knees. He was purchased at five by Margaret Wilson, as her first horse. Pre-purchase X-rays of *Puncheon's knees showed he should be able to jump 2'6" without too much problem. Keeping his damaged knees in mind, she brought him along slowly, always being prepared to stop schooling at the first evidence of trouble, but there were no impediments to his progress. The pair never looked back, winning the South Jersey show circuit Working Hunter Year End Championship in 1974. The high point of their show career was winning a Reserve Championship at the Devon Horse Show in 1977, after campaigning in Maryland, New Jersey and Pennsylvania.

In 1980 Margaret married. Her husband, who had never ridden, learned to ride on the patient "Poochie" and again in 1982 the gelding won the South Jersey circuit Working Hunter Championship with his pupil in the saddle.

Although Margaret stopped jumping "Poochie" when he was 17, at twenty-five he is not retired. She still rides and practices a little dressage with him.[15] (Photo Courtesy Robert A. Moseder)

---

[15] Margaret Wilson Derascavage, English Creek, New Jersey, letter, May 1, 1990.

Sartoris Winning the 3-Foot Jumper Class at the
Bath Horse Show, Robert Wyatt up. *(Photo courtesy Robert Wyatt)*

Sir Olton (*Chadwicke Manor-Miss Tolton by Tintagal) a bay gelding of 1960 was purchased as a four-year-old maiden at Thistledown Race Track near Cleveland, Ohio for $100. Later that year he was sold to Gingr Vaughn of Kent, Ohio who rode him for pleasure. From Gingr, Sir Olton went to the Robert Wyatts of Bath, Ohio where his successful show career as Sartoris began. For several years, he competed nearly every weekend in a Central Ohio Horseshows Association show winning, "Zillions of classes with a wide variety of riding students of all ages."[17] During this period he also worked as a school horse. Sartoris won the Jay Lemmon Memorial Class (equitation) four times with each of the Wyatt children, David, Tom (twice) and Annie in 1981 at the age of 21. In 1976, he was C.O.S.C.A. High Point Hunter Under Saddle Champion and Reserve Champion Junior Hunter Under Saddle while carrying neighbor Diana Reed to the C.O.S.C.A. Hunter Equitation Championship, an honor he also won with Linda Gallagher in the saddle.

---

[17] Susie Wyatt, Bath, Ohio, letter, May 1990

The elegant Sea Wolf *(Photo courtesy of Margaret Kaiser)*

MIGHTY DEEP (Great Depths-Broken Roe by Warrior Nelson) foaled in 1973 made 49 starts in three seasons of racing at Fairmount Park in Collinsville, Illinois. He won twice, was second four times, and eleven times third for earnings of $8,851. At five, he was purchased by Jane Myre, who renamed him Sea Wolf and trained him for eventing, reaching the Preliminary level. He also served as Jane's hunting horse. After a short time as an open jumper, Sea Wolf was sold at age twelve to Kitty Mollman for her daughter Melanie, who was then fifteen. They became a successful pair under the tutelage of John Korenak of Irish Fox Stable in St. Louis. Melanie qualified with him for the AHSA Medal her last three years as a junior rider before leaving for college. It was decided to sell Sea Wolf to another junior rider, but before the sale was completed, he was cast in his stall and dislocated his hip. Showing the Thoroughbred courage to fight back against catastrophic illness, Sea Wolf made a splendid recovery. His veterinarian advised against subjecting the injured hip to much stress. Sea Wolf was then leased to John Korenak, his former trainer, to be used lightly as a lesson horse. John gradually brought him back to good condition by patient and careful training. The gelding now gives lessons to both beginners and more advanced hunt seat riders. He seems to know how to treat riders at each level, "very mellow with rank walk-trot kids, and much more lively with those who can handle it. Both Melanie and I still enjoy riding him when we can, and he is a much loved member of our family."[18]

---

[18] Kitty Mollman, St. Louis, Missouri, Letter, May, 1990.

The legendary Snowbound with William Steinkraus aboard.
Photo courtesy Clive Hiles

Gay Vic (Hail Victory - Gay Alvena by Gay World) 1958, was unplaced in 5 starts at 2 and bowed in both forelegs without earning a cent. He was sent to Mrs. Barbara Worth Oakford, a prominent California trainer of jumpers, to be started over fences. Renamed Snowbound, the gelding showed unusual natural talent as a jumper and was bought by John Galvin of Santa Barbara who donated him to the United States Equestrian Team. One of the mainstays of the team, Snowbound, ridden by Bill Steinkraus, won top international jumping competitions all over the world, including the gold medal at Mexico City in 1958, the first Olympic Gold Equestrian Medal won by the U.S.

USET coach Bert de Nemethy described him as "the best coordinated, bravest, most confident jumper I have ever witnessed."[19] Snowbound served eight years as a USET horse competing at the international grand prix level.

Another former racehorse on the USET was Helen's Vino (Vino Puro-Helen Abrigail by War Glory) 1951, unplaced in 19 starts. Renamed Sinjon, he was ridden both by Bill Steinkraus and by George Morris. Sinjon was the team's leading performer in Europe in 1962 until he went lame at the Olympics in Tokyo.[20]

---

[19] Harlan Abbey, "Substitute Careers," *The Thoroughbred Record,* Lexington, Kentucky, September 5, 1969.
[20] Ibid.

Stuart Little, Laurie Masto up, winners of six consecutive Hunter Classics on the "A" circuit in California. *(Photo by Stock Photography)*

Racing at Bay Meadows, Gifted Hunter (Hunting Party-Exalted Gift by Exalted Rullah), a bay gelding foaled in 1984, was a model of consistency at two. In three starts in 1986, he was never in the hunt, being content to gallop near the back of the pack, finishing as much as 29-1/2 lengths off the pace.

As a show horse, however, he lived up to his registered name. Purchased in 1989 at the age of five from Flintridge Riding Club for 12 year-old Laurie Masto, he was renamed Stuart Little in honor of the protagonist of E.B. White's classic by that name. "A pleasant, debonair little character", described the fictional character's namesake accurately. Laurie and Stuart immediately clicked as a winning combination; "it was love at first sight for both."[20] The pair immediately began garnering ribbons and championships in hunter and hunt seat equitation classes at A circuit AHSA shows up and down the Pacific Coast. Of the eight Hunter Classics Laurie and Stuart entered, they won the blue in the last six consecutive, after placing in the first two. The Hunter Classics are so very popular that the entries are limited to 50 participants.

---

[21] Adelle Masto, Arcadia, California, Letter, May 1990.

SUNNYBROOK

Sunnybrook (Grey Eagle-Sweet Rececca by *Grounded II) a 16:1 grey gelding foaled in 1976, made 4 starts in the only year in which he raced earning $368. He changed hands several times before being bought as a ten-year-old by Bess Reineman of Nashville, Tennessee as a dressage prospect. He has been shown successfully through Fourth Level and is now schooling Prix St. Georges at which level Bess plans to show him during the summer of 1990. In 1988 he was Fourth in the A.H.S.A. Zone IV Horse of the Year Awards and has several Third Level awards in both the Georgia Dressage Association and the Dixie Dressage Association. In 1989 in Lexington, Virginia he was third at Fourth Level at a five ring show with 750 entries; he had numerous other successful shows which qualified him for the AHSA Finals.21 (Photo courtesy Bess Reineman)

---

22 Bess Reineman, Nashville, Tennessee, Letter, May, 1990.

A Favorite Teacher

Jester Princess (Jester-Princess of Agra by Sailor) won at Belmont and Aqueduct. She is now a dependable school horse at Friendship Stables in Palmyra, Virginia.

WARP FACTOR WON

The dark bay or brown Thoroughbred mare Warp Factor Won (Windy Tide-Screaming Jet by Jet Age), a foal of 1976, was bought as an unraced two-year-old in training by Teresa and Bill Nootenboom of Canby, Oregon. Teresa is a former race track groom and exercise rider. She has also trained Arabs for show, but for her own use, prefers Thoroughbreds. Warp Factor Won has proved to be an extraordinarily versatile performer, winning in halter, pleasure driving, trail and both English and Western pleasure classes. She has also been ridden in many parades where she is always quiet and dependable. She was voted Most Versatile Thoroughbred in the Thoroughbred Exhibitors' Association's Year End Championships in 1982, 1983, 1984 and 1986.[24] (Photo courtesy J. Bortvedt Photography.)

---

[24] Teresa Nootenboom, Canby, Oregon, letter, May 1990

Chapter 16

A Short History of the Thoroughbred

The Thoroughbred was developed in England from racing stock imported from Arabia, Turkey, Egypt and from the Barbary Coast of North Africa. The names of the early foundation sires usually designated their national origin; they were variously known as Arabs, Turks or Barbs, although of the same desert-bred ancestry.

Although it is well established that the breed's foundation sires were purebred Arabs of the highest quality, it is less commonly recognized that the foundation mares were also principally of Arabian ancestry. The mares in England before the Eastern importations were either draft or pony type (which Lady Wentworth in her monumental *Thoroughbred Racing Stock* describes as a "coarse-fibred, phlegmatic, thick-skinned, slow breed."[1] Their influence upon the development of the breed is negligible.

The increase in height of the Thoroughbred over its Arabian ancestors has often been attributed to crossing with the native English stock. In light of the refinement of type that the Thoroughbred has maintained throughout its history, this assumption seems to be improbable. The increase in size from an average of 13:3 hands (55 inches) in 1700 to almost 16 hands (64 inches) at the present time has been effected by better

---

[1] Lady Wentworth, *Thoroughbred Racing Stock and It's Ancestors*, George Allen & Unwin, Ltd., London, 1938, p17.

nutrition and selective breeding. Increased nutrition leads to increased size, as diminished nutrition results in stunting. It is hard to imagine an environment more conducive to the nurture of horses than that of England. The damp, mild climate encourages good grazing and forage, while the limestone subsoil on which the grasses grow and from which drinking water flows in wells and springs encourages the development of good bone. The Arabian horse's small stature was due, at least in part, to the arid condition of his homeland. Where food was limited for both man and animal, a small horse was more efficient than a large one and having lesser needs, could survive where a large one would have perished.

In breeding for racing excellence, increase in size was a natural consequence of selection, since the good big horse can almost always beat the good little horse. Therefore, the quite extraordinary growth in size in about 26 generations, over a time span of something less than 300 years, is attributable to improved nutrition and to the selection for racing speed, which favors size. It is probable that increase in size has reached its limit; the giant Thoroughbred is likely to be less agile and less sound than the average of the breed, though of course there are exceptions.

Essentially, the Thoroughbred is a highly specialized Arab developed for its racing qualities - speed, courage and stamina. Many of the greatest Thoroughbreds retain Arabian characteristics to a marked degree: large, prominent, round, wide-set eyes are typical of the best individuals; like his desert ancestor, the modern Thoroughbred has one, or sometimes two, fewer lumbar vertebrae and two fewer pairs of ribs than the common horse.

The development of the breed reflects the history of England. In the days of heavy armor, heavy horses of the Dutch or Flemish type were required. The rout of the French at Agincourt (1414) by British bowmen marked the end of the era of the armored knight mounted on the armored Great Horse. The whole concept of the function of cavalry changed from that of a ponderous and invincible juggernaut, capable of crushing anything in its path by sheer brute force, to that of the swift raider that could make a rapid, thrusting attack and an equally swift withdrawal. A light horse, almost as tall as the Great Horse but maneuverable and speedy was sought. Henry VIII made laws (about 1540) in the hope of increasing the size of England's horses, many of which were pony size. There are no records of how long the rigid enforcement of elimination for size by compulsary slaughter lasted.[2] But his methods were negative, rather than constructive. He issued an edict that all horses under 14 hands be slaughtered and imposed heavy fines for the keeping of undersize horses. No consideration was given to breed or type, height being the only criterion.

Although there was horse racing during the Tudor Era (1485-1603), it was among the slow, cumbersome horses available at the time. In fact, it is likely that wherever horses and men have coexisted there has been horse racing; accounts of matches in England go back to the ninth century and the reign of Athelstan. It was not until the Arabian importations, however, that a true breed of running horse began to evolve.

Horse racing has been known as "The Sport of Kings" and it is to the kings of England that the world owes credit for the development of the Thoroughbred. From the time of Henry VIII (reigned 1508 to 1547) to Elizabeth II, British monarchs have taken an avid and active interest in horses, racing and breeding.

By the seventeenth century, English roads had improved so greatly that travel by wheeled vehicles was possible; the need for more and better horses was acute. But by contemporary accounts, the native horses of England were described as being "vile and ordinary," "widge beasts," and "worthless and despicable."[3]

The Crusaders had brought back from the Near East tales of the legendary horse of the desert which was unmatched for beauty, tractability, courage, hardiness, stamina and speed. Arabian horses were brought to England in increasingly great numbers from the early seventeenth century. Some animals were legitimately purchased through merchants and dealers, or

---

[2] Lady Wentworth, *loc. cit.,* p. 115.
[3] *Ibid.* p. 156

directly from the Bedouin tribesmen. Others, such as the Byerly Turk and the Lister Straddling Turk, captured in Hungary at the siege of Buda in 1687, were taken as the spoils of war.

The most important importations, those which figure most prominently in present day pedigrees, were made between 1625 and 1730. Although other Arabs continued to be brought into the country, the later importations were not of as much consequence in developing the breed because the English racehorse was already superior to the stock from which it had sprung. With increased height and greater speed, the development of the Thoroughbred had become, even at that early date, independent of the parent breed.

In their native land, Arabian horses were inbred to a degree that most modern breeders would not dare duplicate. The homozygous background of the Arab made not only for a uniformity of type, but also for a high degree of prepotency. Purity of bloodlines was carefully guarded and a mare which had once been bred by a common or impure stallion was no longer considered to be Kehilan. The word Kehilan means "purebred all the way through," or "Thoroughly bred;" the word "Thoroughbred" derives from it, although the term did not come into general use until the nineteenth century. The expressions "blooded," "of the blood," "blood-horse," "of the best blood" and "clean bred" have been used at various times to describe the English racehorse.

The first Arab of record to be imported to England and sold to James I was known as the Markham Arabian, named for the merchant who brought him to the British Isles in 1616. As was the custom of the day, a horse was called by his owner's name, by the horse's place of origin or purchase, or by some outstanding physical characteristic. Unfortunately, the practice had a tendency to create confusion, since horses often changed name with each change in ownership.

The Markham Arabian was described as a small bay horse. Although he proved to be a disappointment as a runner, he was kept as a royal stallion and was probably the sire of the unbeatable racehorse Mackerel. After 30 years, the descendants of the Markham Arabian dominated the Royal Stud at Tutbury.

After the execution of Charles I in 1649, the Roundheads seized and confiscated the Royal Stud, dispersing it in 1651. "Roundhead" was a derisory term applied to the puritanical anti-royalists during the Civil War 1642-51; they were so called because they wore their hair closely clipped in contrast to Cavaliers who took foppish pride in their long curls. In 1654, Oliver Cromwell, leader of the Roundheads, outlawed all racing, fearing that race courses would become meeting grounds for royalist sympathizers who wished to see the monarchy restored. He died of malaria in 1658.

In 1660, Charles II returned from exile in Holland to assume the British throne. The Restoration marked a blossoming of the arts suppressed during the puritanical Interregnum. Theatre, painting and music all underwent a renaissance; pleasure was no longer equated with sinfulness. Mirth and buffoonery dominated the court[4]. Racing finally came into its own.

Charles II, known as "the father of the British Turf," often rode his own horses in races. It was during his reign (1660-1685) that the area around Newmarket became the center for racing and breeding. According to tradition, one of his first acts was to set about rebuilding the Royal Stud. It is legend that he sent his Master of Horses to the Middle East to procure race mares for breeding. It is more likely that they were purchased from dealers and importers from France and Italy. Funds were said to have been spent "without count." The mares obtained by Charles II and their daughters were subsequently known as Royal Mares and were so designated in the stud books of the day. During the same period, Louis XIV (1643-1715) was importing Arabs to France; the Royal Mares in that country were branded with an "L" and a crown. The famous Godolphin Arabian came to England by way of France.

The earliest of the great foundation sires was the Byerly Turk. He was captured from the Turkish forces at the siege of Vienna by Captain Byerly who later rode him in Ireland in King

---

[4] W.E. Lunt, *History of England*, Harper & Brothers, New York, 1928, p. 458

William's War, including the decisive battle of Boyne where the English were victorious over the Irish secessionists in 1691. The horse was a beautiful bay with a round, prominent eye, arching neck and high head carriage. As a sire, he proved to be extraordinarily prepotent, getting progeny of great quality. He is the founder of one of the three extant male lines, through his grandson Herod, from whom descended such turf greats as Tourbillon, *Ambiorix, *My Babu, and more recently Amber Morn, Crozier, Inverness Drive and Precisionist. The Byerly Turk is also a strong influence through his daughters, especially the Byerly Turk mare, also called Treasure, the tap root dam of Bruce Lowe's Family No. 3. (A discussion of Bruce Lowe follows later in this chapter).

One of the major influences on the development of the breed was the Leedes Arabian. In certain pedigrees, his importance in sheer bulk is double that of the Darley and Godolphin Arabians combined, yet he left no enduring direct male line. He was brought to England toward the end of the seventeenth century and described as having a very dark, almost black, seal brown coat color, marked only on a near hind pastern. He was purchased by Queen Anne in 1705.

The most famous of the old foundation sires, the Darley Arabian, was purchased in 1703 in Aleppo, a city in Syria, as a three year old by Thomas Darley, whose name he bears. The horse was of the Managhi strain, which the Arabian tribesmen prized for its beauty, speed and endurance. The second of the great male lines traces from him through his great-great grandson, the undefeated Eclipse from which descend the overwhelming number of modern Thoroughbreds including: Ben Brush, *Rock Sand, Bend Or, Ariel, Domino, Sweep, Hampton, Hyperion, *Alibhai, *Teddy, *Bull Dog, *Sir Gallahad III, *Khaled, Swaps, Eight Thirty, Nearco, *Nasrullah, Bold Ruler, Pharlaris, Secretariat, Spectacular Bid, Seattle Slew, Foolish Pleasure, Spy Song, Dr. Fager, Nashua, Mill Reef, Habitat, Northern Dancer, Brigadier Gerard and *Nijinsky II.

In his portrait by J. Sartoris, Sr., the Darley Arabian appears as an elegant, airy creature with a small, beautifully formed head at the end of a graceful, swan-like neck. A bright bay, marked with a narrow blaze and three white feet, he stood an even 15 hands (60 inches), an extraordinary height for the time. He lived to a great old age, purportedly well into his thirties and tradition holds that he was still siring foals as late as 1733. In direct male line, his descendants outnumber both other foundation sires by a great preponderance, although their influence outweighs his.

All gray Thoroughbreds trace in unbroken, though not direct line to the Alcock Arabian foaled in 1704. During his lifetime he was variously known as the Alcock, Pelham or Ancaster Arabian and as the Akaster Turk, reflecting his changes of ownership and the vagaries in spelling of the records of the time. He may also have been the same horse as the Honeywood Arabian and the Holderness Turk! He was imported from Constantinople by Sir Robert Sutton. Since gray is epistatic to all other coat colors, a gray horse must have at least one gray parent; once the color is lost to a breed it can never be regained, except from outside influences. At one time, the color had almost been eliminated from the Thoroughbred breed because it had fallen into disfavor in England. Fortunately, however, it was preserved in France and was re-established in England by the gray stallion Roi Herod, sire of the Tetrarch; the latter sired Tetratema, known as "the Wonder Horse" who got *Royal Minstral, one of the prominent sires in the United States in the 1930's. The Tetrarch also sired Mumtaz Mahal, dam of Mah Mahal, producer of *Mahmoud, winner of the 1936 Derby Stakes at Epsom in record time. *Mahmoud became a major influence on the breed. In this family of horses, the gray color was reputed to be a corollary of speed, the gray individuals excelling those of other coat colors.

The exceptional performance of the "Gray Ghost of Sagamore", Native Dancer, who met defeat only once in 22 career starts while competing against the best horses of his time, would seem to bear out the above theory. In his only loss, he suffered very bad racing luck in the 1953 Kentucky Derby, in which he finished second to Dark Star. Native Dancer descends from the Alcock Arabian through his fourth dam, *La Grisette by Roi Herod. Native Dancer's son Raise a Native displayed his sire's brilliance at two, winning all of his starts, three of them stakes races while setting two new track records and equalling one he had broken previously. Raise a Native was a chestnut as was his brilliant son Majestic Prince, winner of the Kentucky Derby and the Preakness Stakes, while another son of Raise a Native, Mr. Prospector, the sire of earners of over $37,976,981 through 1989, the sire of 93 stakes winners and the most sought after sire in the world, is a bay. So much for predicting performance by coat color!

Europe's greatest breeder of Thoroughbreds, Frederico Tesio, at whose Dormello Stud in Italy such champions as Nearco and *Ribot were bred, called gray coat color a "disease" or an inherited defect. Rather than a true coat color, it is thought to be an inherited characteristic, superimposed upon other colors, resulting in what Tesio referred to as "a premature senility of the coat"[5] and disordered pigmentation. The incidence of melanomas, which are pigmentented tumors occurring in aged gray horses would seem to lend credence to his theory.

Orange, also called Darcy's Yellow Turk, was a chestnut and is believed to be responsible for the introduction of that coat color among the bay foundation sires. The chestnut color is recessive and thus may be carried hidden for many generations.

Last of the great progenitors of the Thoroughbred to be imported to England was the Godolphin Arabian, called after one of his owners, Lord Godolphin, the era's foremost breeder of racing stock. The horse came to England by way of France, imported by Edward Coke about 1730. He was kept at Mr. Coke's stud in Derbyshire, Longford Hall, until his owner's death in 1733. The horse passed through the hands of a London horse dealer before going to the second Earl of Godolphin. He stood at the Godolphin stud, Babraham in Cambridgeshire until his death on Christmas Day in 1753, at the approximate age of twenty. Sham or Shami ("Syrian"), as he was known during his lifetime, was a bay with a heavily crested neck. According to the veterinary surgeon Osmer who saw him

---

[5] Federico Tesio, *Breeding the Racehorse*, translated by Edward Spinola, J.A. Allen & Company, London, 1958, p.82

in his prime, ". . .his shoulders were deeper and lay further into his back than any horse as yet seen. Behind the shoulders there was but a very small space before the muscles of his loins rose excessively high, broad and expanded, which were inserted into his quarters with greater strength and power than in any horse I believe ever seen of his dimensions."[6]

Many legends, some more fanciful than others, grew up around him, including the probably apocryphal tale of his pulling a water cart through the streets of Paris. Most of the fictions about him, this, as well as the celebrated battle with the stallion Hobgoblin, were perpetrated by one Eugene Sue, a writer of lurid novelettes, whose tales of the horse's life were accepted as gospel by subsequent writers.

The Godolphin Arabian's immediate descendants were uniformly excellent and of the true Arabian type. His male line continues through his grandson Matchem to whom trace in direct descent such notables as Spendthrift, Hastings, Fair Play, Man O'War, Chance Play, Grand Slam, Seven Hearts, Display, War Admiral, Olden Times, Intentionally, In Reality, Believe It and Almamoon.

Much less is known about the mares which were imported during the same time than is known about the stallions. The mares were most often designated simply as to place of origin, such as Arabian Mare or Barb Mare; there was inevitably a great deal of duplication and at least five different mares are simply described as Natural Barb mare. Mares were also known by their sires, such as the Byerly Turk Mare or Akaster Turk mare (of which there are at least two), or by some outstanding physical characteristic such as Old Bald Peg who had a very wide blaze, or Bloody Buttocks, a gray with remnants of impermanent chestnut foal hair on her quarters. There was also a stallion by the latter name.

In the latter part of the 19th century, Bruce Lowe, an Australian, traced every mare then in the General Stud Book back in tail female to her original ancestress in the first volume of the General Stud Book. He found that although there were 100 mares in the first volume of the Stud Book, only 50 survived

---

[6] Wentworth, *op.cit.* p. 187

in direct bottom, or female line. The other 50 mares had no surviving progeny in direct descent. Lowe gave the foundation mares numbers, designating each as a "family" as a female counterpart to the male sire lines. The greatest number of Derby, St. Leger and Oaks winners trace to Family No. 1: Tregonwell's Natural Barb Mare. Family No. 2 had the second largest number of Derby, St. Leger and Oaks winners, and so on. The Lowe system makes a convenient way for classifying female descent.[7]

Snorting Bess, or Tregonsell's Natural Arabian Mare, is the tap root ancestress of Family No. 1. A gray, she was also called Place's White Arabian or Turk Mare.

The bay Arabian mare Old Bald Peg was foaled about 1665. She is the progenitrix of Bruce Lowe's Family No. 6 and is one of the most important influences upon the Thoroughbred. She saturates modern pedigrees, far outweighing the influence of any of the foundation sires.

The Old Morocco Mare, a daughter of Old Bald Peg, is another important influence in her own right. Burton's Barb Mare, a bay, is another strong influence. She is the founder of Family No. 2; although called "Barb" she was undoubtedly an Arab of the highest type.

The first Arabian importations to the British Colonies in North America were made from England, while, later, horses were brought directly from North Africa and the Middle East. Although the Thoroughbred had been produced extensively in North America since colonial times, breeders relied upon continuous importation of European stock. In recent times, however, the flow of bloodstock has been reversed as the United States has become the principal reservoir of high quality racing strains.

By tradition, the first stallion imported to the New World was *Bulle Rock to Virginia in 1730, at the age of 21. He was reputed to be by the Darley Arabian. Others followed: *Dabster and *John Baylor's Crab. *Monkey arrived in 1747; although 22 that year, he sired 300 foals in his remaining time at

---

[7] Sir Charles Leicester, *Bloodstock Breeding*, J.A. Allen & Company, London, 1957, p. 62 et seq.

stud.[8] *Jolly Roger, *Morton's Traveller, *Janus and *Fearnaught were other early imports. Mares of high quality, as well, were imported by the New York, Virginia and Maryland gentry, many of whom had received their education at English schools and universities. Among the mares were *Queen Mab, *Selima and *Betty Leedes, said to be the dam of True Briton, allegedly the sire of Justin Morgan, the progenitor of the breed which bears his name.

The development of racing in the colonies was similar to that in England a century before. Since by 1750 the Thoroughbred was fairly well established as a breed in England, better racing stock was available for American racing enthusiasts to build upon than had been available to the British a century earlier.

In the early days, no general breeding records had been maintained. Under James I public race courses had been established where contests of three and four mile heats were held; although the names and descriptions of the winners were kept, no record was made of their pedigree. The individual studs kept breeding records, some more assiduously than others, but the confusion arising from the changes and duplication of names rendered the accuracy of the early records questionable at best.

In 1727 John Cheney began compiling race records under the inclusive title *An Historical List or Account of All the Horse-Matches Run and of All the Plates and Prizes Run for in England (of Ten Pounds or Upward)*. After Cheney's death, his work was continued by Reginald Heber and later still by William Tuting and Thomas Fawconer who called their publication The Sporting Calendar. In 1773 it was taken over by James Weatherby; to this day it is still the property of the Weatherby family.

In compiling an *Introduction to a General Stud Book*, James Weatherby drew from Cheney's records and from the private records which had been kept by the various studs. Only horses whose ancestors traced in all branches were eligible for inclusion in the Thoroughbred stud books; in England Arabs and Anglo-Arabs (a cross between a Thoroughbred and an

---

[8] Roger Longrigg, *The History of Horse Racing,* Stein and Day, New York, 1972, p. 108

Arab) are recorded in a section of the General Stud Book; in the United States, registration of Arabs and Anglo-Arabs was discontinued in 1943. In England, Anglo-Arabs and Arabs are still recorded in the General Stud Book, provided both parents are included therein. Since 1978, the Arab Horse Society has also assumed the task of registering Arabs and Anglo-Arabs to race. The association also oversees a broad spectrum of Arab racing at various race courses throughout Britain. [9]

In England, an Anglo Arab filly, Lilias, won the Oaks in 1826; Exhibitionist, also an Anglo-Arab, was second in the Epsom Derby. In more recent times, Chip, an Anglo-Arab gelding, won 22 races, was second 19 times and 12 times third. Horses of mixed pedigree - and sometimes the imperfection is many generations removed - are issued a certificate for racing only when they come to the United States.

In 1913 the Jersey Act was passed by the English Jockey Club. The act was aimed specifically at preventing an influx of American racing and breeding stock to compete, presumably, to the detriment of local horses. The act decreed that henceforth a horse was ineligible for registration in the stud book, unless it traced in all its lines to animals which had already been recorded in the General Stud Book. This act demoted most American Thoroughbreds to half-bred status, including the illustrious Man O'War, because many mares had left England for North America before the General Stud Book had been initiated. English Thoroughbreds trace in female line to one of the recognized tap root mares such as Snorting Bess, Old Bald Peg or Burton's Barb Mare while most American families are less specifically designated as Mare by *Fearnaught, the *Janus Mare, for example. The Jersey Act was amended in 1949 so that horses for whom it was possible to prove eight or nine generations of pure blood lines might be accepted. In recent years, The American Stud Book took a somewhat similarly dim view of horses from South America which sometimes have an undocumented mare in the outer reaches of their pedigrees.

The end product of centuries of selective breeding based

---

[9] *A Guide to Arab Racing,* Arab Horse Society, Ramsbury, England, 1990, p. 1.

almost solely upon performance, has been the development of an animal unmatched for courage, intelligence and speed. The Thoroughbred has been adversely criticized for being high strung, thin-skinned and brittle, but it is hard to say to what extent the imputed defects are attributable to hard use before the horse has reached maturity.

The Thoroughbred shares with his Arabian ancestors certain definite and unique physical characteristics: the position of the eye in the skull (low, rather than high), the shape of the orbit and eye (round eye set in a round orbit rather than a triangular appearing eye set in a triangular orbit), the rectangular, rather than square interdontal space; smaller teeth, greater bone density, fewer lumbar vertebrae and ribs than the common horse. Wide frontal bones are a corollary to a short back, occurring in many of the best individuals.

The term "hot blood," is more than a figure of speech. The composition of a Thoroughbred's blood differs from that of an ordinary or "cold blooded" horse in that it has a higher percentage of red blood cells. . ."hemoglobin level, red cell count and packed cell volume are significantly higher in the Thoroughbred."[10] It is the red blood cells which carry oxygen from the lungs to other body cells; the higher red cell count of the Thoroughbred helps account for the superior athletic accomplishments.

From England, Thoroughbreds were sent all over the world. "English Horse" was at one time used synonymously with "Thoroughbred". In all countries, Thoroughbreds have been used to improve the local strain of horse for sport or military purposes, as well as being kept pure for racing. Ireland, France, Canada, The United States, Italy, Germany, Hungary, Russia, South Africa, Kenya, Argentina, Brazil, Chile, Ecuador, Hong Kong, Australia, New Zealand and Japan all have an active Thoroughbred racing and breeding industry.

The Thoroughbred has been the foundation of all the American breeds of light horse, with the exception of the Appaloosa and of the Thoroughbred's own parent stock, the

---

[10] J. D. Steel, B.V. Sc., "Hematology and Its Relationship to Track Performance," *Equine Medicine and Surgery*, Santa Barbara, California, 1963, p. 404.

Arab. The Thoroughbred, Denmark, is the foundation sire of the American Saddle Horse, as *Messenger is of the Standardbred. The Morgan Horse is another offshoot of the Thoroughbred and, in turn, profoundly influenced the Standardbred, Saddlebred and Tennessee Walking Horse. The Quarter Horse originally developed from imported English racing stock in colonial days; the breed acknowledges *Janus as its foundation sire. In the interim, there was an infusion of other blood from Chickasaw Indian ponies in the Colonial Period, draft, Mustang, Morgan and of others of unknown background. The Quarter Horse still relies on repeated infusions of Thoroughbred blood to maintain its racing quality, most notably from the Thoroughbred Three Bars (Percentage-Myrtle Dee by Luke McLuke 1940) and his sons.

The Quartermaster Corps of the United States Army was responsible for procuring suitable horses for the cavalry. Production of light horses in the United States declined in both quality and quantity in the early years of the 20th century, a situation which lead to difficulty in obtaining a steady supply of military horses. In 1913, the Remount Service was initiated as a branch of the Quartermaster Corps to encourage farmers to breed more and better horses. By offering farmers the services of superior stallions at a nominal fee, increased production of more useful horses was assured. The need for larger, faster, more athletic horses favored the use of Thoroughbred stallions over stallions of other breeds.

Because of their speed, high courage and most particularly because of their ability to improve upon the grade mares to which they were bred, Thoroughbred stallions were maintained throughout the United States by the Army Remount Service to insure a steady supply of high quality military horses. Stallions were loaned to responsible agents, without charge, for use on their own mares, as well as to service mares belonging to others for a nominal fee, not to exceed ten dollars. The remount depots at Front Royal, Virginia; Fort Robinson, Nebraska; Fort Reno, Oklahoma; and Pomona, California also conducted a limited breeding operation for the purpose of instructing Army personnel in breeding procedures. Thus they could properly supervise the handling of the leased stallions by the various agents; to test new stallions for fertility before placing them with agents; and to provide superior animals for special purposes which could not have been purchased within the rather low purchase price set by government regulations.

One of the last horses bred for the Olympic Team by the U.S. Remount Service was Democrat (Gordon Russel-Princess Bonby), foaled at Fort Robinson, Nebraska in 1933. Ridden by Colonel (subsequently General) Franklin F. Wing, Democrat won the jumper championship at Madison Square Gardens in 1940. In 1948, he placed fourth individually at the Olympic Games in London. He was a member of the U. S. Team that won the Nations Cup in Lucerne and in Dublin; he also won individual classes at Aachen and White City. He continued to compete at the top level until his retirement at 18 years of age.[11] The 1940's saw the end of the military Olympic Teams which were replaced by civilian teams. But the influence continued. Trail Guide, one of Hugh Wiley's Olympic Team mounts was a product of the Remount Service breeding program. He competed at the International level while in his late teens.

Mounted troops of the United States Cavalry last saw action in the Bataan Campaign of World War II in 1942 when the 26th Cavalry Regiment (Philippine Scouts) was annihilated by the Japanese.

In 1949, all remaining cavalry horses were sold, except those over 17 years of age who lived out their days at Fort Riley, Kansas. At Fort Myer, Virginia, which adjoins Arlington Cemetary, horses are maintained for parades and for military funerals in which they pull the caissons.

The high regard in which the Army Remount Service held

---

[11] John Strassburger, "Great Jumpers of the Past," *The Chronicle of the Horse*, Middleburg, Virgina, March 2, 1990, p. 4.

TRAIL GUIDE

The Thoroughbred, Trail Guide, Hugh Wiley up at the 1956 Olympic Games in Stockholm. Trail Guide was the leading U.S. Equestrian Team horse in two Olympics. The U.S. Team finished fifth overall in Stockholm. Trail Guide was 18 years old at that time. (Photo courtesy Hugh Wiley.)

the Thoroughbred is reflected in the number of Thoroughbred stallions maintained compared with those of other breeds. The following figures are of December 1, 1943: of 606 stallions placed with 493 agents nationwide, at 73 depots or area head quarters, 569 stallions were Thoroughbreds, while only 37 were of all other breeds combined. Many of the better grade horses in the United States are the result of the Army's up-breeding program. Records were kept by the Remount Service until it was disbanded in 1944.

The demise of the Cavalry and the discontinuation of the Remount Service marked the end of a proud, historic era. While no one could mourn an end to the slaughter of horses in war, it was sad to see the termination of the services both agencies provided to American horsemen. The Cavalry School at Ft. Riley, Kansas, set a standard for equitation and training which improved horsemanship nationwide. The Cavalry also trained farriers to a high level of skill at both Ft. Riley and for the horse drawn artillery at Ft. Sill, Oklahoma. The Remount Service, by making available the services of well-bred stallions for a mere pittance, succeeded in improving the overall quality of American horses to an outstanding degree.

Boots and Saddles has been sounded for the last time; the caissons go rolling along only between Ft. Myer and Arlington Cemetary.

Thoroughbred Breeder's & Owner's Organizations[1]

American Thoroughbred Breeders Alliance, P. O. Box 427, 201 W. Padonia Road, Timonium, MD 21093. (301) 252-2100.

Arizona Thoroughbred Breeders Association, P. O. Box 41774, Phoenix, AZ 85080-1774. (602) 942-1310.

Arkansas Thoroughbred Breeders Association, P. O. Box 1665, Hot Springs, AR 71902. (501) 624-6328.

California Thoroughbred Breeders Association, P. O. Box 750, Arcadia, CA 91006. (818) 445-7800.

Canadian Thoroughbred Horse Society
  Ontario Division: P. O. Box 172, Rexdale, Ont., Canada M9W 5L1.
  (416) 675-3602.
  Alberta Division: 410-1501 1st Street, S.W., Calgary, Alb.,
  Canada T2R 0W1. (403) 226-2248.
  British Columbia Division: 17687 56-A Ave., Surrey, B.C.
  Canada V3S 1G4. (604) 574-0145.
  Saskatchewan Division: R.R. 5, Hill Street, Saskatoon, Sask.,
  Canada S7K 3J8. (306) 374-7777.

Florida Thoroughbred Breeders Association, 4727 North West 80th Avenue, Ocala, FL 32675. (904) 629-2160

Georgia Thoroughbred Owners & Breeders Association, 8 Piedmont Center, Suite 105, Atlanta, GA 30305. (404) 261-1541

Horsemen's Benevolent & Protective Association, Inc., 2800 Grand Route, Saint John Street, New Orleans, LA 70119. (504) 945-4500

Idaho Thoroughbred Breeders Association, 5000 Chinden Blvd., Suite A, Boise, ID 83714. (208) 375-5930.

Illinois Thoroughbred Breeders & Owners Foundation, P. O. Box 1990, Fairview, IL 62208. (618) 344-3427

Thoroughbred Association of Indiana, P. O. Box 2472, West Lafayette, IN 47906. (317) 447-3986

Kentucky Thoroughbred Owners & Breeders, Inc., P. O. Box 4158, Lexington, KY 40544. (606) 277-1122

Louisiana Thoroughbred Breeders Association, P. O. Box 24650, New

---

[1] *The Blood-Horse Directory of North American Racing and Breeding-1990*, The Blood-Horse, Lexington, KY., 1990.

Orleans, LA 70184. (504) 947-4676

Maryland Thoroughbred Horsemen's Association, Inc., 6314 Windsor Mill Road, Baltimore, MD 21207. (301) 265-6842

Michigan United Thoroughbred Breeders and Owners, P. O. Box 2752, Livonia, MI 48151. (313) 422-2044.

Minnesota Thoroughbred Association, 13755 Nicollet Avenue, S., Suite 200, Burnsville, MN. 55337. (612) 892-6200

National Steeplechase & Hunt Association, P. O. Box 308, Elmont, NY 11003. (516) 437-6666

Nebraska Thoroughbred Breeders Association, Inc., P. O. Box 2215, Grand Island, NE 68802. (308) 384-4683

Thoroughbred Breeders and Owners Association of New Jersey, 231 Crosswicks Road, Bordentown, NJ 08505. (609) 298-6401.

New York Thoroughbred Breeders, Inc., 287 Hempstead Turnpike, Elmont, NY 11003. (516) 354-7600.

North Carolina Thoroughbred Association, Rt. 8, Box 225, Mocksville, NC 27028. (919) 998-5724

Ohio Thoroughbred Breeders and Owners, 920 Race Street, Suite 201, Cincinnati, OH 45202. (513) 241-4589

Oklahoma Thoroughbred Association, 100 N.W. 63rd, Suite 200, Oklahoma City, OK 73116. (405) 840-3712.

Oregon Thoroughbred Breeders Association, P. O. Box 17248, Portland, OR 97217. (503) 285-0658.

Pennsylvania Horse Breeders Association, 203 N. Union Street, Kennett Square, PA 19348. (215) 444-1050.

Tennessee Thoroughbred Owners and Breeders Association, Suite 1300, Plaza Tower, Knoxville, TN 37929. (615) 637-7777

Texas Thoroughbred Breeders Association, P. O. Box 14967, Austin, TX 78761. (512) 458-6133

Thoroughbred Owners and Breeders' Association, P. O. Box 4158, Lexington, KY 40544. (606) 276-2299

Virginia Thoroughbred Association, 38 Garrett Street, Warrenton, VA 22186. (703) 347-4313

Washington Thoroughbred Breeders Association, P. O. Box 88258, Seattle, WA 98138. (206) 226-2620

West Virginia Thoroughbred Development Fund, P. O. Box 551, Charles Town, WV 25414. (304) 725-7001

North American Thoroughbred Racetracks

AGUA CALIENTE, S.A., Boulevard Agua Caliente, Tijuana, B.C., Mexico. 22420 (011) 81-78-11

AK-SAR-BEN, Ak-Sar-Ben Field, Omaha, NE 68106 (402) 556-2305

ALBUQUERQUE, P. O. Box 8510, Albuquerque, NM 87198. (505) 262-1188

AQUEDUCT, P. O. Box 90, Jamaica, NY 11417. (718) 641-4700

ARLINGTON RACE TRACK, LTD., P. O. Box 7, Arlington Heights, IL 60006. (312) 255-4300

ASSINIBOIA DOWNS, P. O. Box 10, Station A, 3975 Portage Avenue, Winnipeg, Manitoba, Canada R3K 2C7. (204) 885-3330

ATLANTIC CITY RACE COURSE, P. O. Box 719, Atlantic City, NJ, 08404. (609) 641-2190

ATOKAD PARK, P. O. Box 518, South Sioux City, NE 68776. (402) 491-4502

BALMORAL PARK, P. O. Box 158, Crete, IL 60417. (312) 568-5700

BAY MEADOWS, P. O. Box 5050, San Mateo, CA 94402. (415) 574-7223

BELMONT PARK, P. O. Box 90, Jamaica, NY 11417. (718) 641-4700

BEULAH PARK, 3664 W. Grant Avenue, P. O. Box 6, Grove City, OH 43123. (614) 871-9600

BLUE RIBBON DOWNS, P. O. Box 788, Sallisaw, OK 74955. (918) 775-7771

CALDER RACE COURSE, INC., P. O. Box 1808, Carol City Branch, Opa-Locka, FL 33055. (305) 625-1311

CANTERBURY DOWNS, 1100 Canterbury Road, P. O. Box 508, Shakopee, MN 55379. (612) 445-7223

CHARLES TOWN, P .O. Box 551, Charles Town, WV 25414. (304) 725-7001

CHURCHILL DOWNS, INC., 700 Central Avenue, Louisville, KY 40208. (502) 636-4400

COLUMBUS, Platte County Agricultural Society, P. O. Box 1335, Columbus, NE 68602-1335. (402) 564-0133

DELAWARE PARK, P. O. Box 6008, Wilmington, DE 19804. (302) 994-2521.

DEL MAR, Del Mar Thoroughbred Club, P. O. Box 700, Del Mar, CA 92014. (619) 755-1141

DELTA DOWNS, P. O. Box 188, Vinton, LA 70668. (318) 589-7441

DETROIT RACE COURSE, Ladbroke Racing Corporation, 28001 Schoolcraft Rd., Livonia, MI 48150. (313) 525-7300

EL COMANDATE, El Comandante Operating Co., P. O. Box 1675, Canovanas, PR 00629. (809) 724-6060

ELLIS PARK, P. O. Box 33, Henderson, KY 42420 (812) 425-1456

EVANGELINE DOWNS, U.S. Highway 167 North, P.O. Box 90270, Lafayette, LA 70509-0270. (318) 896-7223

EXHIBITION PARK, Vancouver, British Columbia, Canada V5K 3N8. (604) 254-1631

FAIR GROUNDS, 1751 Gentilly Boulevard, P. O. Box 52529, New Orleans, LA 70152. (504) 944-5515

FAIRMOUNT PARK, Rt. 40, Collinsville, IL 62234. (618) 345-4300

FAIRPLEX PARK, P. O. Box 2250, Pomona, CA 91769-2250. (714) 623-3111

FERNDALE, Humbolt County Fair Association, P. O. Box 637, Ferndale, CA 95536. (707) 786-9511

FINGER LAKES, P. O. Box 364, Canandaigua, NY 14424. (716) 924-3232

FONNER PARK, P. O. Box 490, 700 East Stolley Park Road, Grand Island, NE 68802. (308) 382-4515

FORT ERIE, P. O. Box 1130, Station B, Ft. Erie, Ontario, Canada (416) 871-3200

FRESNO, 1121 Chance Avenue, Fresno, CA 93702. (209) 453-3247

GARDEN STATE PARK, Rt. 70 and Haddenfield Road, P. O. Box 4274, Cherry Hill, NJ 08034-0649. (609) 488-8400

GOLDEN GATE FIELDS, P. O. Box 6027, 1100 Eastshore Freeway, Albany, CA 94706. (415) 526-3020

GRANTS PASS, P. O. Box 282, Grants Pass, OR 97526. (503) 476-1639

GREAT FALLS, P. O. Box 1524, Great Falls, MT 59403. (406) 727-8900

GREENWOOD, The Ontario Jockey Club, P. O. Box 156, Rexdale, Ontario, Canada M9W 5L2. (416) 698-3131

GULFSTREAM PARK, 901 S. Federal, Hallandale, FL 33009. (305) 454-7000

HARBOR PARK, P. O. Box 1229, Elma, WA 98541. (206) 482-2651

HAWTHORNE, 3501 South Laramie Avenue, Cicero, IL 60650. (312) 242-1350

HIALEAH PARK, P. O. Box 158, Hialeah, FL 33011. (305) 885-8000

HIPODROMO DE LAS AMERICAS, Lomas de Sotelo, Mexico 10, D.F. Mexico. (905) 557-4100

HOLLYWOOD PARK, P. O. Box 369, Inglewood, CA 90306. (213) 419-1500

JEFFERSON DOWNS, INC., P. O. Box 640459, Kenner, LA 70064. (504) 466-8521

JUAREZ RACE TRACK, P. O. Box 1349 Ciudad Juarez, Chih., Mexico. (915) 778-6322

KEENELAND, P. O. Box 1690, 4201 Versailles Road, Lexington, KY 40592-1690. (606) 254-3412 or (800) 456-3412.

LA MESA PARK, P. O. Box 1147, Raton, NM 87740. (505) 445-2301

LAUREL RACE COURSE, P. O. Box 130, Laurel, MD 20725. (301) 725-0400

LES BOIS PARK, 5610 Glenwood Road, Boise, ID 83714 (208) 376-7223.

LINCOLN, Nebraska State Fair Park, P. O. Box 81223, 1800 State Fair Park Drive, Lincoln, NE 68501-1223. (402) 474-5371.

LONGACRES RACE COURSE, P. O. Box 60, Renton, WA 98057. (206) 226-3131

LOS ALAMITOS RACE COURSE, 4961 Katella Avenue, Los Alamitos, CA 90720. (714) 751-3247.

LOUISIANA DOWNS, 8000 East Texas Street, P. O. Box 5519, Bossier City, LA 71171-5519. (318) 742-5555.

MARQUIS DOWNS, P. O. Box 8428, Saskatoon, Sask., Canada S7K 6C7. (306) 242-6100

MARSHFIELD FAIR, P. O. Box 5, Marshfield, MA 02050. (617) 834-6629

THE MEADOWLANDS, East Rutherford, NJ 07073. (201) 935-8500

METRA PARK, P. O. Box 2514, Billings, MT 59103. (406) 256-2400

MONMOUTH PARK, P. O. Box MP, Oceanport, NJ 07757. (201) 222-5100

MOUNTAINEER PARK, P. O. Box 358, Chester, WV 26034. (304) 387-2400

NORTHAMPTON, P. O. Box 305, Fair Street, Northampton, MA 01060. (413) 584-2237

NORTHLANDS PARK, P. O. Box 1480, Edmonton, Alberta, Canada T5J 2N5. (403) 471-7379

NUEVO LAREDO DOWNS, P. O. Box 164, Nuevo Laredo, Tamaulipas, Mexico. (871) 401-11

OAKLAWN PARK, P. O. Box 699, Hot Springs, AR 71902. (501) 623-4411

PENN NATIONAL RACE COURSE, P. O. Box 32, Grantville, PA 17028. (717) 469-2211

PHILADELPHIA PARK, P. O. Box 1000, Bensalem, PA 19020-2096. (215) 639-9000

PIMLICO RACE COURSE, Maryland Jockey Club, Baltimore, MD 21215. (301) 542-9400

PLAYFAIR RACE COURSE, P. O. Box 2625, Spokane, WA 99220. (509) 534-0505

PLEASANTON, 4501 Pleasanton, Pleasanton, CA 94566. (415) 846-2881

PORTLAND MEADOWS, 1001 North Schmeer Road, Portland, OR 97217. (503) 285-9144

PRAIRIE MEADOWS, 1 Prairie Meadows Drive, Altoona, IA 50009-0901

(501) 967-1000.

PRESCOTT DOWNS, P. O. Box 952, Prescott, AZ 85302 (602) 445-0220

REGINA, Regina Exhibition Park, P. O. Box 167, Regina, Sask., Canada S4P 2Z6. (306) 527-2674

REMINGTON PARK, 301 North West 63rd Street, Suite 340, Oklahoma City, OK 73116. (405) 424-1000.

RILLITO RACE TRACK, 4502 N. 1st Avenue, Tucson, AZ 85718 (602) 293-5011.

RIVER DOWNS, 63401 Kellogg Avenue, P. O. Box 30286, Cincinnati, OH 45230. (513) 232-8000

ROCKINGHAM PARK, P. O. Box 47, Salem, NH 03079. (603) 898-2311

RUIDOSO DOWNS, P. O. Box 449, Ruidoso, NM 88346. (505) 378-4431

SACRAMENTO, California Exposition and State Fair, P. O. Box 15649, Sacramento, CA 95842. (916) 942-2089

SALEM FAIRGROUNDS, 2330 17th Street North East, Salem, OR 97310. (503) 378-3247

SANDOWN PARK, 837 Burdette Avenue, Victoria, British Columbia, Canada V8W 1B3. (604) 386-2261

SAN JUAN DOWNS, Lee Acres, CPO Box H, Farmington, NM 87401. (505) 326-4551

SANTA ANITA, Santa Anita Park, Arcadia, CA 91007. (818) 574-7223

SANTA FE DOWNS, Rt. 14 Box 199 RT, Santa Fe, NM 87505. (505) 471-3311

SANTA ROSA, P. O. Box 1536, Santa Rosa, CA 95402. (707) 545-4200

SARATOGA, P. O. Box 564, Saratoga Springs, NY 12866 (518) 584-6200

SOLANO, 900 Fairgrounds Drive, Vallejo, CA 94589. (707) 644-4401

SPORTSMAN'S PARK, 3301 South Laramie Avenue, Cicero, IL (312) 242-1121

STAMPEDE PARK, P. O. Box 1060, Station M, Calgary, Alberta, Canada T2P 2K8. (403) 261-0214

STOCKTON, P. O. Box 6310, Stockton, CA 95206. (209) 466-5041

SUFFOLK DOWNS, P. O. Box B, East Boston, MA 02128. (617) 567-3900

SUN DOWNS, P. O. Box 6957, Kennewick, WA 99336. (509) 582-5434

SUNLAND PARK, 101 Futurity Drive, Sunland Park, NM 88063. (505) 589-1131

TAMPA BAY DOWNS, P. O. Box 2007, Oldsmar, FL 34677. (813) 855-4401

THISTLEDOWN, 21501 Emery Road, North Randall, OH 44128. (216) 662-8600

TIMONIUM, Maryland State Fair, P. O. Box 188, Timonium, MD 21093. (301) 252-0200

TURF PARADISE, 1501 West Bell Road, Phoenix, AZ 85023. (602) 942-1101

TURFWAY PARK, 7500 Turfway, Florence, KY 41042. (606) 371-0200

WHOOP-UP DOWNS, 3401-6 Ave. South, Lethbridge, Alberta, Canada T1J 1G6. (403) 328-4491

WOODLANDS RACECOURSE, 9700 Leavenworth Road, P. O. Box 12036, Kansas City, KS 66112. (913) 299-9797.

WOODBINE, P. O. Box 156, Rexdale, Ontario, Canada M9W 5L2. (416) 675-6110

WYOMING DOWNS, P. O. Box 1607, Evanston, WY 82931. (307) 789-0511.

YAKIMA MEADOWS, P. O. Box 213, Yakima, WA 98907. (509) 248-3920

Appendix III

Sales Companies

Barretts, P. O. Box 2010, Pomona, CA 91769. (714) 629-3099.

California Thoroughbred Sales, Inc., P. O. Box 201, Colorado Place, Arcadia, CA 91006. (818) 445-7753.

Fasig-Tipton Company, Inc., 2400 Newtown Pike, Lexington, KY 40583 (606) 255-1555. Conducts sales in various locations in the United States.

Equivest Breeders' Sales Company, P. O. Box 55, Somers Point, NJ 08244. (609) 484-2833.

Keeneland Association, Inc., P. O.Box 1690, 4201 Versailles Road, Lexington, KY 40592. (606) 254-3412. Conducts yearling, breeding stock and mixed sales at beautiful Keeneland Race Course in Lexington.

Heritage Place, Inc., 2829 South MacArthur Blvd., Oklahoma City, OK 73128. (405) 682-4551.

Ocala Breeders' Sales Company, P. O. Box 99, Ocala, FL 32678. (904) 237-2154.

Woodbine Sales, P. O. Box 156, Rexdale, Ontario, Canada M9W 5L2. (416) 674-1460

Additionally, many of the regional breeders associations conduct yearling and mixed sales.

Appendix IV

Registries, Publications & Associations

Registries

The Jockey Club, 821 Corporate Drive, Lexington, KY 40503. (800) 444-8521. The keepers of the American Stud Book.

Weatherby & Sons, 7 Cross Street, W. York LS22 4RT, England. The keepers of the British Stud Book

Thoroughbred Publications

The Blood-Horse, 1736 Alexandria Drive, Box 4038, Lexington, KY 40544. (606) 278-2361. A weekly magazine covering racing, breeding, sales, farm management and veterinary topics.

The Chronicle of the Horse, P.O. Box 46, Middleburg, VA 22117. (703) 687-6341. The horse in sport: hunting, eventing, showing. Published weekly.

Practical Horseman, Gum Tree Corner, Unionville, PA 19375. (215) 857-1101. How to articles on training, stable management, grooming, first aid, conformation, equitation, breeding and foot care. Published monthly.

Spur, P.O. Box 85, Middleburg, VA 22117. (703) 687- 6314. The Thoroughbred in sport-racing, hunting, 'chasing, polo breeding, personalities; lavishly illustrated in color. Published bimonthly.

The Thoroughbred Times, P. O. Box 8237, Lexington, KY 40533. (606) 223-9800. Weekly tabloid format, news of racing, breeding, sales and veterinary items

Most of the local Thoroughbred breeders and owners associations publish newsletters and magazines. A letter or phone call to your nearest Thoroughbred Association office will probably get you a free sample. Most of these publications exist to advertise local farms and stallions; they print news of local race meetings, local legislation, locally bred horses which have succeeded in the real world; with few exceptions, they are of only parochial interest. *The Maryland Horse* and *The Thoroughbred of California* are both excellent magazines which do not fall into the narrow confines described above. They offer well-written articles of general interest to horsemen nationwide on bloodlines, training methods and veterinary subjects.

Horsemen's Associations

The American Horse Council, 1700 K Street, N.W., Suite 300, Washington, DC 20006. (202) 296-4031

The American Horse Shows Association, Inc., 220 East 42nd Street, New York, NY 10017. (212) 972-2472

The Green Mountain Horse Association, South Woodstock, VT 05071. Maintains a complete equestrian center, sponsors the original Hundred Mile Trail Ride, the model for other competitive and endurance rides which followed it.

The Thoroughbred Exhibitors Association, 24174 South Log House Road, Colton, OR 97017. This is a group "dedicated to the promotion of the Thoroughbred as an all round, versatile athlete with the heart and physical ability to be a champion in any horse activity." The group sponsors family trail rides and gives year-end awards for points gained in driving, dressage, western pleasure, hunter, jumper and equitation classes, endurance and competitive trail rides and combined training.

U.S. Pony Clubs, Inc., 893 S. Matlack Street, Suite 110, West Chester, PA 19382. (215) 436-0300. An organization dedicated to teaching children between the ages of 7 and 21 to become competent riders in the areas of dressage, jumping and eventing. The term "pony" refers to the age of the rider not the size of the horse.

National 4-H Council, 7100 Connecticut Avenue, Chevy Chase, MD 20815. (301) 961-2944.

United States Dressage Federation, Inc., P.O. Box 80668, Lincoln, NE 68501. (402) 474-7632.

United States Combined Training Association, Inc. 292 Bridge Street, South Hamilton, MA 01982. (508) 468-7133.

Many states also have a state Horse Council dedicated to the promotion of the horse industry in that state; sponsoring trail rides, shows, three-day events, and other exhibitions. They also conduct seminars and other educational opportunities for horsemen of all breeds. Your local tack shop or horse supply business will have information as to the Horse Council's location and activities.

UNIVERSITY AFFILIATED MEDICAL CENTERS by REGION

EAST

Equine Study Coordinator
Cornell University
Box 135, B-12 Ives Hall
Ithaca, NY 14853 (607) 255-4987

University of Pennsylvania
Kennett Square, PA 19104
(215) 444-5800

Tufts University
North Grafton, MA 02111.
(617) 956-7600.

SOUTH

Auburn University
Auburn, AL 36849.
(502) 826-4000

University of Florida
Gainesville, FL 32601
(904) 392-3261

University of Georgia
Athens, GA 30602
(404) 542-3030

Louisiana Tech Equine Center
Box 19187TS
Ruston, LA 71272
(318) 257-4024

Mississippi State University
Mississippi State, MS 39762
(601) 325-2131

North Carolina State University
Raleigh, NC
(919) 829-4212

University of Tennessee
Knoxville, TN 37901
(615) 974-0111

Texas A & M University
College Station, TX 77843
(713) 845-2311.

Tuskeegee Institute
Tuskeegee, AL 36088
(205) 727-8011

Virginia-Maryland Regional
College of Veterinary Medicine
Blacksburg, VA 24061
(703) 961-7911

Marion duPont Scott Equine Medical Center
Leesburg, VA 22075
(703) 771-6800

MIDWEST

University of Illinois
Urbana, IL 61801
(217) 333-1192

Iowa State University
Ames, IA 50011
(515) 294-8657

Kansas State University
Manhattan, KS 66502
(913) 532-6011

Michigan State University
East Lansing, MI 48824
(517) 355-1855

University of Minnesota
St. Paul, MN 55108
(612) 373-2851

Ohio State University
Columbus, OH 43210
(614) 422-6446

Purdue University
West Lafayette, IN 47907
(317) 494-7613

University of Wisconsin
Madison, WI 53706
(608) 256-9810

FAR WEST

University of California-Davis
Davis, CA 95616
(916) 752-1011

Colorado State University
Fort Collins, CO 80523
(303) 491-1101

Oklahoma State University
Stillwater, OK 73111
(405) 624-6961

Oregon State University
Corvallis, OR 97331
(503) 754-0123

Washington State University
Pullman, WA 99164
(509) 335-9515.

Index